2.2

Hello, Reader!

Think of all the things you learn when you read! In this book, you will read many exciting stories. Meet a funny dog with a serious job. Watch amazing ants up close. Take a spin on a dream carousel.

As you read, you will meet characters that try to help others and characters that have special talents.

**Enjoy all the Delights
in these stories.**

HOUGHTON MIFFLIN
Reading

Delights

Senior Authors
J. David Cooper
John J. Pikulski

Authors
Patricia A. Ackerman
Kathryn H. Au
David J. Chard
Gilbert G. Garcia
Claude N. Goldenberg
Marjorie Y. Lipson
Susan E. Page
Shane Templeton
Sheila W. Valencia
MaryEllen Vogt

Consultants
Linda H. Butler
Linnea C. Ehri
Carla B. Ford

HOUGHTON MIFFLIN
Reading
A Legacy of Literacy

HOUGHTON MIFFLIN   BOSTON • MORRIS PLAINS, NJ

California • Colorado • Georgia • Illinois • New Jersey • Texas

Cover and title page photography by Tony Scarpetta.

Cover illustration is from *Carousel*, by Pat Cummings. Copyright © 1994 by Pat Cummings. Reprinted by permission of Simon & Schuster Books for Young Readers, an imprint of Simon & Schuster Children's Publishing Division. All rights reserved.

Acknowledgments begin on page 411.

Printed in the U.S.A.

ISBN: 0-618-25929-5

9 10 DW 11 10 09 08 07 06 05 04

Amazing Animals 10

folktale

Phonics Library

- A Park for Parkdale
- Arthur's Book
- Hank's Pandas
- Marta's Larks
- Crow's Plan
- Brent Skunk Sings

Big Book

From Caterpillar to Butterfly
by Deborah Heiligman

Outstanding Science Trade Book for Children

On My Way Practice Reader

Sandy Goes to the Vet
by Becky Cheston

Theme Paperbacks

Raptors!
by Lisa McCourt

A Toad for Tuesday
by Russell E. Erickson

Best Books for Children

Family Time 118

realistic fiction

 **Taking Tests**

Phonics Library

- My Sister Joan
- The Big Party Plan
- Lost and Found
- What Will Lester Be?
- Aunt Lizzy Finds Her Cake
- My Brother
- Eight Daughters!
- The Family Garden

Big Book

Liliana's Grandmothers
by Leyla Torres
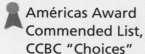 Américas Award Commended List, CCBC "Choices"

On My Way Practice Reader

Swim, Dad!
by Lee S. Justice

Theme Paperbacks

Tonight Is Carnaval
by Arthur Dorros
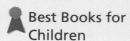 Best Books for Children

Grandaddy and Janetta
by Helen Griffith
 ALA Notable Children's Book, American Bookseller "Pick of the Lists," Best Books for Children

Focus on

Biography

Contents
Theme 6

Talent Show

284

*realistic
fiction*

Phonics Library

- Our Classroom Zoo Book
- Jade's Drumming
- Dwight the Knight
- Who Drew the Cartoon?
- Will Holly Sing?
- Fright Night

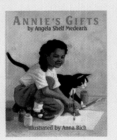

Big Book

Cleveland Lee's Beale Street Band
by Art Flowers

On My Way Practice Reader

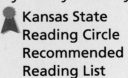

The Garden
by Lee S. Justice

Theme Paperbacks

Annie's Gifts
by Angela Shelf Medearis

🎗 Award-winning author

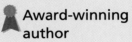

Spotlight on Cody
by Betsy Duffey

🎗 Kansas State Reading Circle Recommended Reading List

Amazing Animals

The Animal Song

Alligator, hedgehog, anteater, bear,

Rattlesnake, buffalo, anaconda, hare.

Mud turtle, whale, glowworm, bat,

Salamander, snail, and Maltese cat.

Polecat, dog, wild otter, rat,

Pelican, hog, dodo, and bat.

Anonymous

Amazing Animals

Contents

Phonics Library

- **A Park for Parkdale**
- **Arthur's Book**
- **Hank's Pandas**
- **Marta's Larks**
- **Crow's Plan**
- **Brent Skunk Sings**

Big Book

From Caterpillar to Butterfly
by Deborah Heiligman

Theme Paperbacks

Raptors!
by Lisa McCourt

A Toad for Tuesday
by Russell E. Erickson

On My Way Practice Reader

Sandy Goes to the Vet
by Becky Cheston

Book Links

If you like . . .

Officer Buckle and Gloria
by Peggy Rathmann

Then try . . .

Martha Speaks
by Susan Meddaugh (Houghton)
When Martha the dog eats alphabet soup, she begins to talk . . . and talk . . . and talk.

Buddy: The First Seeing Eye Dog
by Eva Moore (Scholastic)
A German shepherd becomes famous as the first seeing-eye dog in America.

If you like . . .

Ant
by Rebecca Stefoff

Then try . . .

Chameleon
by Rebecca Stefoff (Benchmark)
An amazing thing about chameleons is that they can change color faster than you can count to ten.

Biggest, Strongest, Fastest
by Steve Jenkins (Houghton)
What animal runs the fastest? Learn fun facts about record holders of the animal world.

The Great Ball Game
by Joseph Bruchac

Then try . . .

The Lizard and the Sun
by Alma Flor Ada (Doubleday)

When the sun disappears in this Mexican folktale, a lizard helps to bring back light to everyone.

A Snake Mistake
by Mavis Smith (Puffin)

In a story based on a real incident, Jake the snake eats light bulbs that he thinks are eggs.

Technology

At Education Place

Post your reviews of these books or see what others had to say.

Education Place®
www.eduplace.com/kids

. . .

At school

Read at school and take a quiz.

Accelerated Reader®

. . .

At home

Read at home and log on to

www.bookadventure.org

15

Safety Officers

Police **officers** who visit schools to talk about **safety** are sometimes called safety officers. In the story you're going to read next, an officer and his partner give safety speeches at an elementary school. Like the **audience** in this story, you should always pay close **attention** to a safety officer's speech. He or she will explain many ways to avoid accidents and to stay safe.

16

Bicycle and In-line Skating Safety

1. Always wear a helmet.

2. Obey traffic signals.

3.

17

FACT FILE

- Peggy Rathmann was born in St. Paul, Minnesota.
- The first time she tried to write a children's book, the book was 150 pages long!
- *Officer Buckle and Gloria* won the Caldecott Medal in 1996.
- Officer Buckle's safety tips are ideas Ms. Rathmann collected from her nieces, nephew, and other children. She gave them each twenty-five dollars for any safety tip she used in the book.

Other books by Peggy Rathmann:
Ruby the Copycat
Good Night, Gorilla

To find out how Peggy Rathmann's dog is a lot like Gloria, take a look at Education Place.

www.eduplace.com/kids

18

PEGGY RATHMANN

Officer Buckle's safety speeches are more exciting than he'd planned. As you read the story, **monitor** how well you understand what happens in it.

Officer Buckle knew more safety tips than anyone else in Napville.

Every time he thought of a new one, he thumbtacked it to his bulletin board.

Safety Tip #77

NEVER stand on a SWIVEL CHAIR.

Officer Buckle shared his safety tips
with the students at Napville School.
Nobody ever listened.
Sometimes, there was snoring.

Afterward, it was business as usual.

Mrs. Toppel, the principal, took down the welcome banner.

"NEVER stand on a SWIVEL CHAIR," said Officer Buckle, but Mrs. Toppel didn't hear him.

Then one day, Napville's police department
bought a police dog named Gloria.

When it was time for Officer Buckle to give
the safety speech at the school, Gloria went along.

"Children, this is Gloria," announced Officer
Buckle. "Gloria obeys my commands. Gloria, SIT!"
And Gloria sat.

Officer Buckle gave Safety Tip Number One:

"KEEP your SHOELACES tied!"

The children sat up and stared.

Officer Buckle checked to see if Gloria was sitting at attention. She was.

"Safety Tip Number Two," said Officer Buckle.
"ALWAYS wipe up spills BEFORE someone SLIPS
AND FALLS!"

The children's eyes popped.

28

Officer Buckle checked on Gloria again.

"Good dog," he said.

Officer Buckle thought of a safety tip he had discovered that morning.

"NEVER leave a THUMBTACK where you might SIT on it!"
The audience roared.

Officer Buckle grinned. He said the rest of the tips with *plenty* of expression.

The children clapped their hands and cheered. Some of them laughed until they cried.

Officer Buckle was surprised. He had never noticed how funny safety tips could be.

After *this* safety speech, there wasn't a single accident.

The next day, an enormous envelope arrived
at the police station. It was stuffed with thank-you
letters from the students at Napville School.

Every letter had a drawing of Gloria on it.

Officer Buckle thought the drawings showed a lot of imagination.

His favorite letter was written on a star-shaped
piece of paper. It said:

You and Gloria make a good team.

Your friend,
Claire

P.S. I always wear
a crash helmet.
(Safety Tip #7)

Officer Buckle was thumbtacking Claire's letter to his bulletin board when the phones started ringing. Grade schools, high schools, and day-care centers were calling about the safety speech.

"Officer Buckle," they said, "our students want to hear your safety tips! And please, bring along that police dog."

Officer Buckle told his safety tips to 313 schools.
Everywhere he and Gloria went, children sat up
and listened.

After every speech, Officer Buckle took Gloria
out for ice cream.

Officer Buckle loved having a buddy.

Then one day, a television news team videotaped
Officer Buckle in the state-college auditorium.

38

When he finished Safety Tip Number Ninety-nine, DO NOT GO SWIMMING DURING ELECTRICAL STORMS!, the students jumped to their feet and applauded.

That night, Officer Buckle watched himself
on the 10 o'clock news.

43

The next day, the principal of Napville School telephoned the police station.

"Good morning, Officer Buckle! It's time for our safety speech!"

Officer Buckle frowned.

"I'm not giving any more speeches! Nobody looks at me, anyway!"

"Oh," said Mrs. Toppel. "Well! How about Gloria? Could she come?"

Someone else from the police station gave Gloria a ride to the school.

Gloria sat onstage looking lonely. Then she fell asleep. So did the audience.

After Gloria left, Napville School had its biggest accident ever. . . .

It started with a puddle of banana pudding . . .

SPLAT! SPLATTER!

SPLOOSH!

Everyone slid smack into Mrs. Toppel, who
screamed and let go of her hammer.

47

The next morning, a pile of letters arrived at the police station.

Every letter had a drawing of the accident.

Officer Buckle was shocked.

At the bottom of the pile was a note written on a paper star.

Officer Buckle smiled.

The note said:

Gloria gave Officer Buckle a big kiss on the nose.

Officer Buckle gave Gloria a nice pat on the back.

Then, Officer Buckle thought of his best safety tip yet....

Safety Tip #101

"ALWAYS STICK WITH YOUR BUDDY!"

Responding

Think About the Selection

1. Choose two safety tips from the story. Explain why they are important.

2. How do Peggy Rathmann's illustrations make this story funny?

3. How do you think Officer Buckle felt when he saw himself on the 10 o'clock news?

4. What does this story teach about teamwork and friendship?

5. Connecting/Comparing In what ways is Gloria an amazing animal?

Expressing

Write a Thank-You Letter

The students at Napville School sent letters to Officer Buckle and Gloria. Write your own thank-you letter. Tell Officer Buckle and Gloria what you thought of their speeches. Tell what you learned about safety.

> **Tips**
>
> • To get started, look at the letters in the story.
> • Be sure to include the date, greeting, closing, and your name.

Make a School Safety Poster

Identify places in your school where safety tips would help. Make a poster showing one of these tips. Be sure to explain why students should follow it.

Present a Safety Tip

Work with a partner. Think of a safety tip that your class should follow. Have one partner act out the safety tip while the other explains it. Can you make your presentation as exciting as Officer Buckle and Gloria's?

Tips

- **Brainstorm a list of possible safety tips.**
- **Look at the class as you present your safety tip.**

Complete a Web Crossword Puzzle

What started with a puddle of banana pudding? Test what you've learned from the story by completing the crossword puzzle on Education Place.

www.eduplace.com/kids

The Story of Owney

from *Postal Pack for Elementary School Students*, National Postal Museum and Smithsonian Institution

More than one hundred years ago, a little dog wandered into a post office and made himself at home among the mailbags. He loved traveling with the mail. Once, when a mailbag accidentally fell off a cart, Owney stayed with the bag to protect it until the postal clerks came back to fetch it.

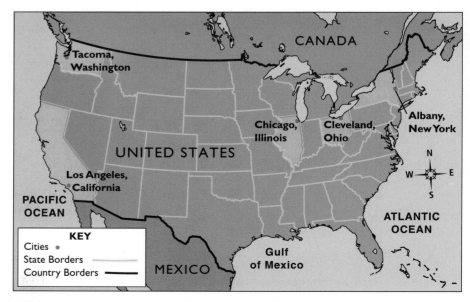

These are just some of the cities Owney visited.

Owney became a famous dog. He jumped onto mail trains whenever he liked. The clerks loved having him along because he was a good luck charm. There was never a railroad accident when Owney was aboard. Wherever he went, postal clerks made a dog tag for him, so others would know where he had traveled. The National Postal Museum has more than one thousand Owney tags that show all the places Owney visited.

Owney loved to ride in the mail cars.

A Research Report

A research report tells facts about a topic in the writer's own words. Use this student's writing as a model when you write a research report of your own.

> The **title** tells what the report is about.

> A **research report** gives **facts** from other sources.

> Writers give the facts in their **own words**.

The Harp Seal

My favorite animal is the harp seal. I've found out a lot about the harp seal that I would like to share with you.

A real harp seal has beautiful gray fur and lives in the cold water in the North Atlantic Ocean. Harp seals are happiest when they are in the water. Their flippers really help them swim quickly. When harp seals are on the icy land, they have to wiggle their bodies so they can move. Their front flippers have claws that help them hold on to the ice and rocks. Mostly they just stay in the water.

When harp seals are in the water they eat shrimp and squid. They also eat big fish. The seals have to be very careful in the water. That's when the polar bears, sharks, and killer whales could swim up and hurt them. Another interesting thing about harp seals is that they don't have ears! They hear sounds through their heads, instead.

The harp seal is very cute, even though it's pretty big. It grows to be six feet long. Someday I would like to see one in person.

A good **ending** wraps up the report.

Meet the Author

Celsey B.
Grade: two
State: Georgia
Hobbies: horseback riding, swimming, and skating
What she'd like to be when she grows up: a horseback rider who jumps or a dentist

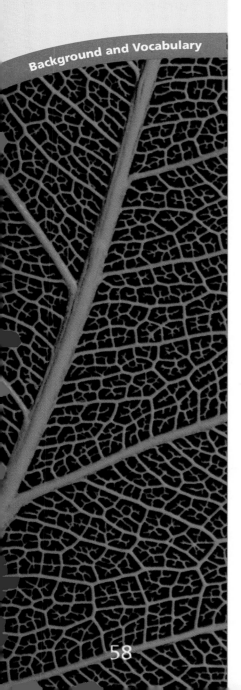

Fun Facts About Ants

Have you ever looked closely at an ant? In the next selection, you'll learn some fun facts about ants from all around the world.

Ants usually live under the ground in groups called **colonies**. Colonies of ants build **tunnels** and store food.

Ants guide themselves inside their tunnels by using the two long **antennae** on their heads.

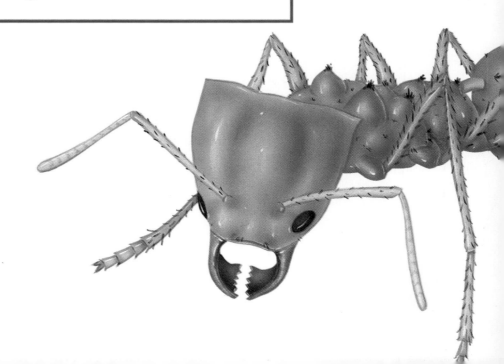

Some ants grow their own food. They eat a special **fungus**, or mold, that they make from leaves.

Young ants, or **larvae**, hatch from **cocoons**.

Meet the Author
Rebecca Stefoff

**Other books by
Rebecca Stefoff:**
Octopus
Owl
Butterfly

Rebecca Stefoff's favorite things to do are traveling and watching animals. She enjoys birdwatching and has traveled all over the world. She has gone scuba diving to observe moray eels, barracuda, and brightly colored coral fish.

When at home in Oregon, she watches the crabs, seals, and shore birds that live nearby.

Ms. Stefoff thinks ants are interesting to watch because they live almost everywhere. "Wherever you go, they're there," she says.

Did you know that one of Rebecca Stefoff's favorite animals is the slug? Find out more about this author by visiting Education Place.

www.eduplace.com/kids

Rebecca Stefoff

ANT

As you read this nonfiction selection, think of **questions** to ask your classmates about the amazing world of ants.

61

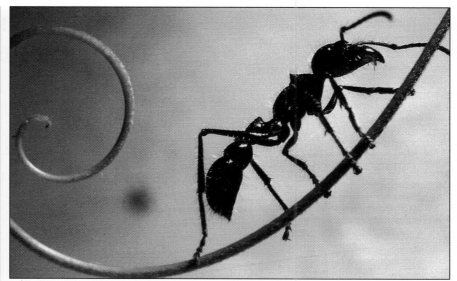

black ant, Costa Rica

Ants.

They're everywhere. You can see ants in almost any part of the world.

But you hardly ever see just one ant. If you see an ant, you will probably find lots of other ants nearby.

anthill, Australia

Ants live and work together in busy, crowded groups called colonies. Most colonies are in tunnels under the ground. The ants carry dirt out of the tunnels to make a pile. We call these piles anthills.

anthill in sidewalk

When you see an anthill in a sidewalk crack, you know there is a city of ants under the sidewalk.

Some anthills are huge and filled with tunnels.
An ant colony has lived under this tree for years.
Each year the ants dig new tunnels and make the
anthill a little bigger.

anthill, East Africa

Every ant has two long, waving stalks on its head. These are its antennae. They are like a nose and fingers all in one.

The antennae tell the ant what is going on around it. They help it find food and then find its way back to its colony.

These two ants are "talking" by rubbing their antennae together. The big ant is the queen. She is the mother of all the ants in the colony. The little ant is a worker. Workers take care of the queen's eggs and bring food to the colony.

red ants transferring food

Ants do all kinds of things together. They pass pieces of food to one another. Sometimes they even carry each other around.

Some jobs are too big for one ant. That's when ants team up. A bunch of little ants working together can carry a big dead bug. It will make a fine meal for the colony.

ants carrying dead stick insect, Brazil

ant bridge, Panama

Ants take a shortcut between tree branches. Some of them hold one another's legs to make a bridge. Others can walk across the bridge to the new branch.

Carpenter ants live in wood. A pile of yellow sawdust on a log means that carpenter ants are busy inside, chewing new tunnels.

Deep in the log, the queen's eggs are turning into larvae. When the larvae hatch from their cocoons, they look like little worms. Later the larvae will turn into ants and pour out of the log.

leafcutter ants, Costa Rica

Leafcutter ants live in Central and South America. Some people call them parasol ants. Do you know why?

The ants chew off pieces of leaves and carry them back to their tunnels. They march with the leaves held over their heads like little sunshades, or parasols.

The ants don't eat the leaves. They chew them into a paste. A yellow fungus grows on the paste, and the ants eat the fungus.

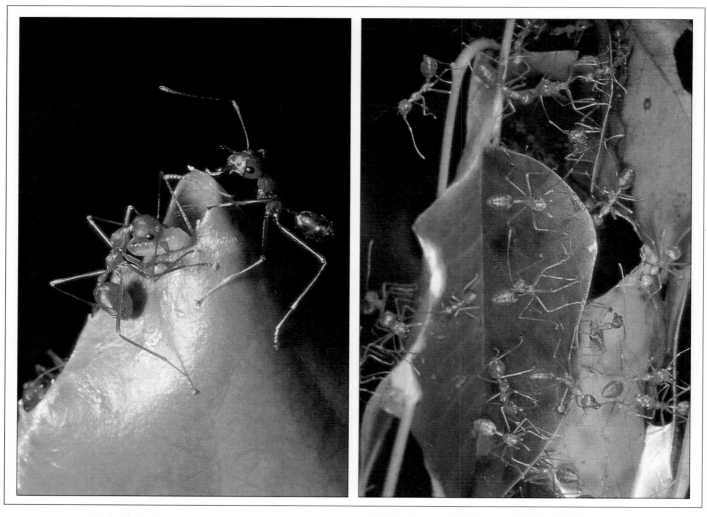

weaver ants with larva   *white larval thread binds leaves*

Weaver ants live in trees in southern Asia and on Pacific islands. They make nests by fastening leaves together with sticky silk thread. The thread comes from the young ants, or larvae. Older ants hold the larvae that spin the thread.

Teams of ants join together into chains to bend the big, stiff leaves.

nest making, Australia

farmer ants with aphids, New York

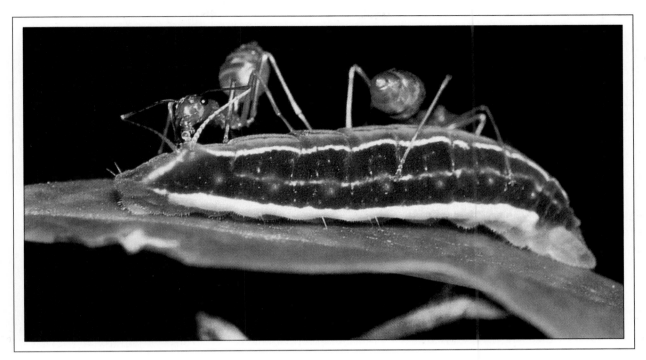

ants "milking" caterpillar

Some ants eat juices that come from inside other insects. They take care of these insects and "milk" them for their juice, like a farmer milks a herd of cows.

The little green bugs are plant eaters called aphids. The ants tending them are called farmer ants.

Army ants live in tropical jungles. They march from place to place, eating plants and insects as they go. They climb right over logs and rocks and even houses.

A colony of army ants on the march covers the ground like a moving, munching carpet. Some colonies are as wide as a street and as long as a city block.

army ants, Costa Rica

A lot of little ants working together can beat one big black beetle. When it comes to teamwork, ants are experts.

Can you pick up your mother and carry her over your head? You could if you were an ant. Ants are very strong. They can carry things that weigh a lot more than they do. It takes only two ants to lift this fat caterpillar.

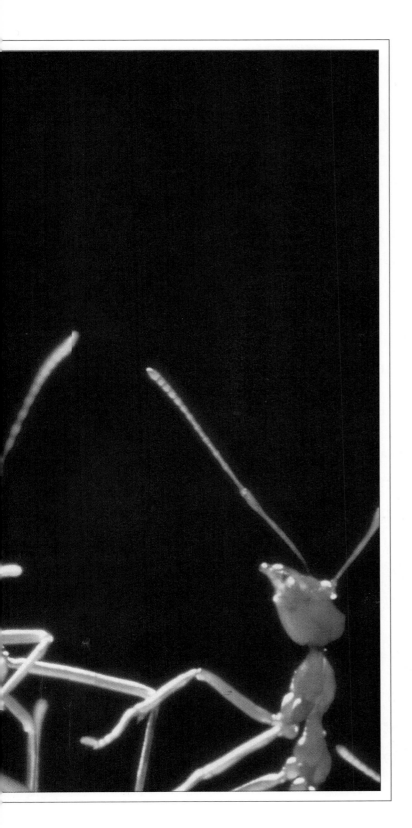

Ants live in colonies that are like cities. They help one another, and they work together on big jobs.

I think ants are a lot like us. Do you?

Responding

Rebecca Stefoff
ANT
LIVING THINGS

Think About the Selection

1. Which facts about ants did you find most amazing?

2. Find three questions the author asks the reader. Why does she ask questions instead of just telling facts?

3. How are ant colonies like cities? Give examples from the selection.

4. In what ways do ants work in teams?

5. **Connecting/Comparing** *Ant* is a nonfiction selection. *Officer Buckle and Gloria* is fiction. Compare the two.

Informing

Write a Report

Choose a type of ant described in the selection. In your own words, write a report that tells facts about the ant that you chose.

Tips

- Use complete sentences.
- Your report should be one or two paragraphs long.

Math

Count Legs

Ants have six legs. If there are five ants on a leaf, how many legs are there in all? Use numbers from the problem to write a multiplication sentence.

Bonus If three more ants climb onto the leaf, how many legs are there in all?

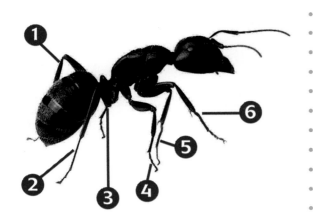

Art

Make Ant Prints

Here's a fun way to decorate a card or plain book cover. Press the eraser end of a pencil into black paint. Print ant bodies on paper. Then draw in the details with a fine-tip black pen. If you want to make red ants, use red paint!

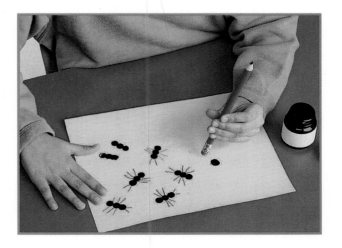

Solve a Web Maze

Help an ant find its way through a Web maze and back to its colony. Print a maze from Education Place, and then fill it in.

www.eduplace.com/kids

Music Link

Skill: How to Read Song Lyrics

1. Skim the **lyrics**, or words of the song, before singing.

2. Sing the first **verse** and then the **chorus**.

3. Repeat for the remaining verses.

The Ants Go Marching
Traditional Children's Song

1. The ants go march-ing one by one, Hur - rah,— Hur - rah.— The ants go march-ing one by one, Hur - rah,— Hur - rah.— The ants go march-ing one by one; The lit - tle one stops to have some fun, and they all go march-ing down in - to the ground to get out of the rain. Boom! Boom! Boom!

86

2. The ants go marching two by two,
   Hurrah, Hurrah. *(repeat)*
   The ants go marching two by two;
   The little one stops to tie his shoe.

   Chorus:
   And they all go marching down into the ground
   to get out of the rain. Boom! Boom! Boom!

3. The ants go marching three by three;
   Hurrah, Hurrah. *(repeat)*
   The ants go marching three by three;
   The little one stops to climb a tree.
   Chorus

4. The ants go marching four by four;
   Hurrah, Hurrah. *(repeat)*
   The ants go marching four by four;
   The little one stops to shut the door.
   Chorus

5. The ants go marching five by five;
   Hurrah, Hurrah. *(repeat)*
   The ants go marching five by five;
   The little one stops to take a dive.
   Chorus

The Great Ball Game

Ball Games

In the story you are about to read, two groups agree to play a ball game in order to end a **quarrel**. Each group believes it has an **advantage** over the other one. Both groups agree that the winners may set a **penalty** that the losers must **accept**.

Ball games have been played in the Americas for hundreds of years.

Native Americans sometimes played these games as a way of settling **arguments**.

One game, which we now call lacrosse, was played with a deerskin ball and long poles that were used to toss the ball.

Meet the Author
Joseph Bruchac

Joseph Bruchac's grandfather, a member of the Abenaki tribe, told him many traditional folk stories. Mr. Bruchac enjoys telling the stories that his grandfather passed on to him, as well as folktales from other Native American tribes.

Meet the Illustrator
Susan L. Roth

Susan L. Roth used cut paper collected from all over the world to make the illustrations for this book: red umbrella paper from Thailand, an envelope from Tibet, blue paper from Japan, and green paper from Italy.

 Internet

To learn more about Joseph Bruchac and Susan L. Roth, visit Education Place.

www.eduplace.com/kids

THE GREAT BALL GAME
◄ A MUSKOGEE STORY ►

RETOLD BY **JOSEPH BRUCHAC**
ILLUSTRATED BY **SUSAN L. ROTH**

Long ago the Birds and Animals had a great
argument.

"We who have wings are better than you," said
the Birds.

"That is not so," the Animals replied. "We who have teeth are better."

The two sides argued back and forth. Their quarrel went on and on, until it seemed they would go to war because of it.

Then Crane, the leader of the Birds, and Bear,
the leader of the Animals, had an idea.
   "Let us have a ball game," Crane said. "The
first side to score a goal will win the argument."

"This idea is good," said Bear. "The side that loses will have to accept the penalty given by the other side."

So they walked and flew to a field, and there they divided up into two teams.

On one side went all those who had wings. They were the Birds.

On the other side went those with teeth. They were the Animals.

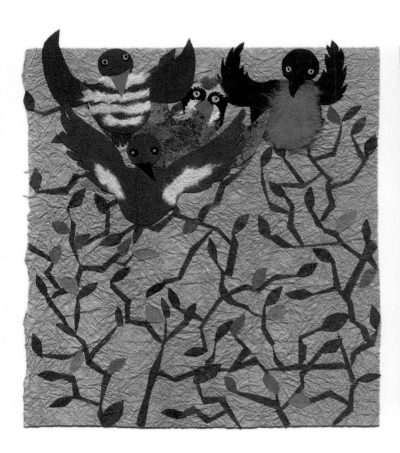

But when the teams were formed, one creature was left out: Bat. He had wings *and* teeth! He flew back and forth between the two sides.

First he went to the Animals. "I have teeth," he said. "I must be on your side."

But Bear shook his head. "It would not be fair," he said. "You have wings. You must be a Bird."

So Bat flew to the other side. "Take me," he
said to the Birds, "for you see I have wings."

But the Birds laughed at him. "You are too little
to help us. We don't want you," they jeered.

Then Bat went back to the Animals. "Please let me join your team," he begged them. "The Birds laughed at me and would not accept me."

So Bear took pity on the little bat. "You are not very big," said Bear, "but sometimes even the small ones can help. We will accept you as an Animal, but you must hold back and let the bigger Animals play first."

Two poles were set up as the goalposts at each
end of the field. Then the game began.

Each team played hard. On the Animals' side
Fox and Deer were swift runners, and Bear cleared
the way for them as they played. Crane and Hawk,
though, were even swifter, and they stole the ball
each time before the Animals could reach their goal.

Soon it became clear that the Birds had the advantage. Whenever they got the ball, they would fly up into the air and the Animals could not reach them. The Animals guarded their goal well, but they grew tired as the sun began to set.

Just as the sun sank below the horizon, Crane
took the ball and flew toward the poles. Bear tried
to stop him, but stumbled in the dim light and fell.
It seemed as if the Birds would surely win.

Suddenly a small dark shape flew onto the field and stole the ball from Crane just as he was about to reach the poles. It was Bat. He darted from side to side across the field, for he did not need light to find his way. None of the Birds could catch him or block him.

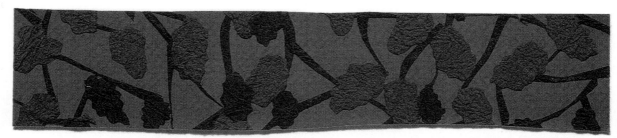

Holding the ball, Bat flew right between the
poles at the other end! The Animals had won!

This is how Bat came to be accepted as an Animal. He was allowed to set the penalty for the Birds.

"You Birds," Bat said, "must leave this land for half of each year."

So it is that the Birds fly south each winter...

And every day at dusk Bat still comes flying to
see if the Animals need him to play ball.

Responding

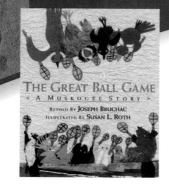

THE GREAT BALL GAME
A MUSKOGEE STORY

RETOLD BY JOSEPH BRUCHAC
ILLUSTRATED BY SUSAN L. ROTH

Think About the Selection

1. What event in nature does this tale explain?

2. How might the story have been different if Bat had not played the game?

3. If Bat had helped the Birds win, what sort of penalty might he have set for the Animals?

4. Do you think the story shows a good way to settle an argument? Why or why not?

5. **Connecting/Comparing** All of the animals in this theme work in teams. Describe each type of team, and then compare two or more teams.

Expressing

Writing a Folktale

Bears go to sleep for the winter. Spiders make webs. Moths fly toward lights. Think of an animal. Write a folktale that explains why the animal acts the way it does.

Tips

- Observe a pet or other animal to get ideas.
- Use a story map to organize your ideas.

110

Science

Make a Fact File

List what you've learned about bats from reading this selection. Then look for information about bats in an encyclopedia or science book. Make a bat fact file using the information you've collected.

Social Studies

Create Game Rules

The Birds and Animals played a game without any written rules. Write a set of rules for them to follow when playing their game. Explain how rules can help them play together fairly.

Take a Web Field Trip

Learn more about amazing animals. Visit Education Place to discover interesting facts about all kinds of animals.

www.eduplace.com/kids

Skill: How to Read a Caption

A caption is a title or short explanation about an illustration or photograph.

• Read the title. This tells you what the illustration or photograph is about.

• Read the labels, or words that tell you about each part.

• Carefully read any other information about the illustration or photograph.

Bat Attitude

from 3–2–1 Contact
by Lynn O'Donnell

Veronica Thomas has been crazy about bats ever since she could walk. Her room is littered with bat puppets, bat key chains, bat books, and glow-in-the-dark bat T-shirts.

Veronica's obsession with bats might have something to do with her dad's job. He's the curator of mammals at the Wildlife Conservation Society (Bronx Zoo) in New York City. Veronica saw her first bat there when she was just a year old.

Batgirl Forever

You might think Veronica wants to be a bat expert when she grows up. But her dream is to become a paleontologist. Paleontologists are scientists who study animal fossils. "Who knows?" says Veronica. "Maybe someday I'll find a fossil of a bat."

Little Brown Bat

The little brown bat of North America is a big eater. In one hour, it can catch and gulp down 600 mosquitoes.

Veronica's Favorite Bat

Straw-colored Flying Fox

Bats on the Brain

Veronica and her dad built a bat house in their backyard. Bat houses give bats a safe place to live and raise a family. Veronica checks it every day for signs of the winged critters.

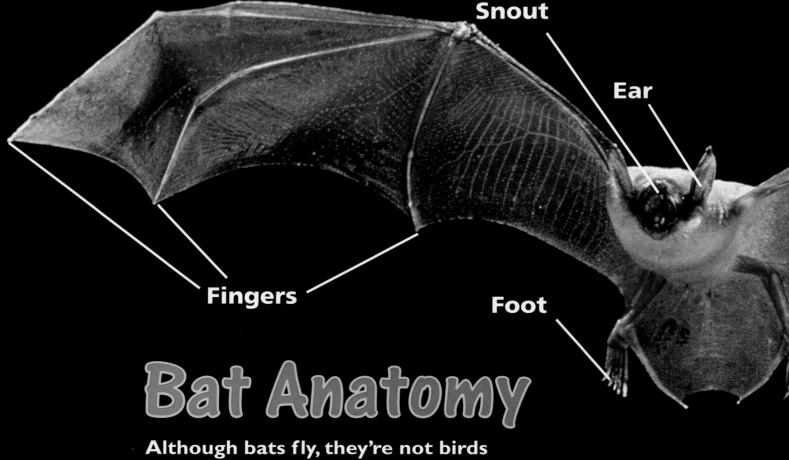

Snout

Ear

Fingers

Foot

Bat Anatomy

Although bats fly, they're not birds — they are mammals.

Make an Origami Bat

. . . .

What you need:
Black or brown construction paper, googly-eyes (optional)

What you do:
First cut paper so that it is a perfect square, equal on all sides.

Then follow the illustrated steps.

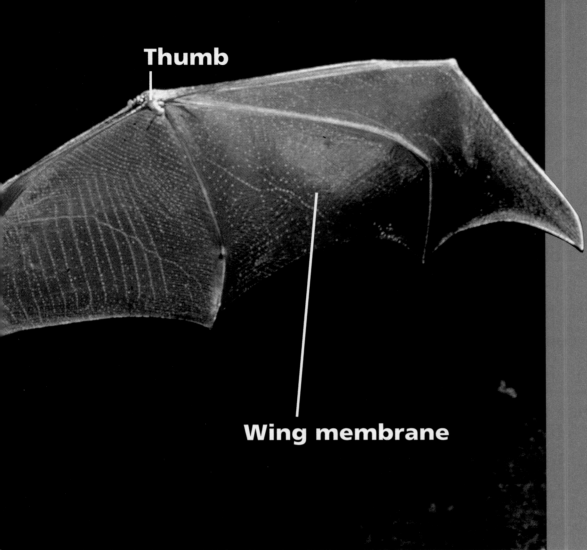

Thumb

Wing membrane

Dinner Call

Bats send out high-pitched sounds. When the sound bounces back off an object, bats can tell if there's food nearby. Some moths send beeps to a bat to trick it. The bat thinks it's found another bat — and the moth doesn't become bat food.

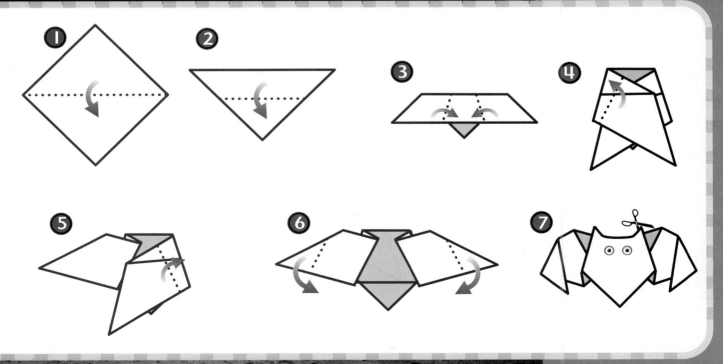

✓ Vocabulary

Some tests ask you to choose the best word to fill in a blank in a sentence. How do you choose the best answer? Below is a sample test item from *Ant*. The correct answers are shown. Use the tips to help you complete this kind of test item.

Read the two sentences. Each sentence has a numbered blank. Choose the word from each list that best completes the sentence.

1   A __1__ ant brings food for the hungry ants in its colony. A big __2__ makes a good meal.

1 ○ queen   ○ green | 2 ○ leaves   ○ nest
   ○ team   ● worker | ● bug   ○ log

Tips
- Read the directions carefully.
- Read the sentences and all the answer choices.
- Fill in the answer circle completely.

Now see how one student figured out the correct answer.

First, I read the sentences and all of the answer choices for each sentence. *Queen* and *team* don't make sense in the first sentence.

The selection doesn't talk about green ants. Only *worker* describes the kind of ant that brings food to the colony. The best answer for the first blank is *worker.*

For the blank numbered **2**, I am looking for a word that describes a good meal for an ant. I know that ants don't eat logs. *Leaves* and *nest* don't make sense in the sentence either. Now I see why *bug* is the best answer.

Family Time

What is a family?
Who is a family?
Either a lot or a few
    is a family;
But whether there's ten
    or there's two in *your* family,
All of your family plus *you*
    is a family!

by Mary Ann Hoberman

119

Family Time

Contents

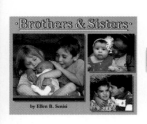

Phonics Library

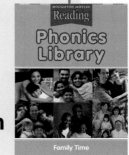

- **My Sister Joan**
- **The Big Party Plan**
- **Lost and Found**
- **What Will Lester Be?**
- **Aunt Lizzy Finds Her Cake**
- **My Brother**
- **Eight Daughters!**
- **The Family Garden**

Big Book

Liliana's Grandmothers
by Leyla Torres

Theme Paperbacks

Tonight Is Carnaval
by Arthur Dorros

Grandaddy and Janetta
by Helen V. Griffith

On My Way Practice Reader

Swim, Dad! *by Lee S. Justice*

Book Links

If you like . . .

Brothers and Sisters
by Ellen B. Senisi

If you like . . .

Jalapeño Bagels
by Natasha Wing

Then try . . .

Then try . . .

Lionel and Louise

by *Stephen Krensky* (Puffin)
Siblings Lionel and Louise do many things together, but don't always do them the same way.

About Twins

by *Shelley Rotner and Sheila M. Kelly* (DK Ink)
Twins may look alike and share a lot, but they are still two different people.

Halmoni and the Picnic

by *Sook Nyul Choi* (Houghton)
Yunmi's grandmother is unsure about America until she chaperones the school picnic.

Henry and Mudge in the Family Trees

by *Cynthia Rylant* (Simon)
Henry's dog Mudge is the most popular guest of all at a family reunion.

If you like . . .

Carousel
by Pat Cummings

Thunder Cake
by Patricia Polacco

If you like . . .

Then try . . .

Then try . . .

Clean Your Room, Harvey Moon!

by Pat Cummings (Simon)

Harvey's mother makes him clean his room.

My Rotten Redheaded Older Brother

by Patricia Polacco (Simon)

Tricia wants to do something better than her brother Richie.

The Birthday Swap

by Loretta Lopez (Lee & Low)

A girl looks for the perfect birthday gift for her sister.

Storm in the Night

by Mary Stolz (Harper)

Thomas and his grandfather talk about thunderstorms.

Technology

Visit www.eduplace.com/kids **Education Place**®

Read at school  **Accelerated Reader**®

Read at home www.bookadventure.org

123

·Brothers & Sisters·

by Ellen B. Senisi

Background and Vocabulary

Being a Brother or Sister

What happens when a **newborn** baby enters a family? In some families, a **teenage** brother or sister may help **grown-ups** take care of younger children.

In the selection you're going to read next, you'll hear brothers and sisters of all ages talk about their families.

Babies and very young children need a lot of attention.

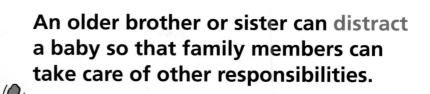

An older brother or sister can distract a baby so that family members can take care of other responsibilities.

Twins are twice the work, and twice as much fun!

Sometimes, a younger sister or brother can seem like a pest. But remember, you were a baby once too.

·Brothers & Sisters·

by Ellen B. Senisi

Brothers and sisters of all ages appear in the next selection. As you read, **evaluate** how well the author uses words and photos to tell their stories.

126

What is it like to have a new brother or sister?
Tori is going to find out soon. Her mother is going
to have a baby. "Is it going to be a boy or a girl?"
Tori wonders. "Will Mommy love me as much when
the baby comes?"

Ben has a newborn brother, and Dorrie has a new sister. Sometimes having a baby in the family is fun.

"Our new baby is so soft and tiny that I want to cuddle her all the time," says Dorrie.

But sometimes a baby is not so much fun.

"Babies can't do anything by themselves," says Ben. "Mommy still loves me. But she is so busy taking care of the baby, I have to play by myself until he takes another nap."

"I'm so tired of hearing everyone say how cute the baby is," says Valerie.

"I like to hold my baby sister all by myself," says Michael. So does Leo.

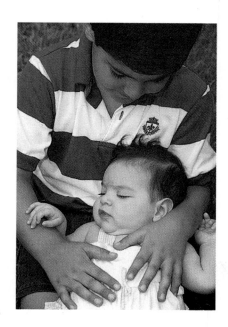

Jasmine and Juanita (hwa-NEE-ta) have baby sisters who have learned how to walk. "She's old enough to get into trouble now," says Jasmine, "lots of trouble."

"I help distract my sister," says Juanita. "My mom says I'm the best helper with the baby."

"My sister always wants to do what I'm doing, but she doesn't play games the way you're supposed to," says Alicia.

"Sometimes," says Judson, "we have so much fun together."

Rena is older than her sister. "I know things my little sister doesn't," says Rena. "Now that she is in kindergarten, I can help her get ready in the morning. And I can take her to her classroom."

"You learn to share when you have a sister," Tori says.

"It's hardest to share our parents," says Rena.

Katelyn and Jordan are almost the same age.
So are Ben and Suzannah.

"Sometimes, we're best friends,"
says Jordan.

"And sometimes we're worst enemies,"
says Katelyn.

Jeremy and Jonathan are twins. "We have each other to play with all the time," says Jeremy.

Ian and Ryan are twins, too. "Dad says that we even sleep the same way," says Ryan. "We like looking so much alike that we can trick people."

"We aren't exactly alike, though," says Ian. "I'm better at drawing, but my brother is better at sports."

Sometimes it's hard to be a younger brother.

"It's not fair!" says Peter. "Just because she's older, my sister can do everything better."

And sometimes it's great to be a younger brother.

"She's my other mom," says Steven.

"We have our own secrets," says Tyler.

"And we have our own special games."

Trey's older brother and Jesse's older sister are both in middle school.

"He gets mad at me because he thinks I'm a pest," says Trey.

"We get mad at each other a lot," says
Jesse. "But then we forget about it."
    "Sometimes, my sister is the only person
who understands how I feel," says Juanita.

Bianca has a teenage sister. "When can I go everywhere and do everything, just like her?" Bianca wonders.

"Sometimes my sister acts like a grown-up, and we don't have anything to talk about," says Maura. "Other times she's just like me."

"I was adopted," says Sujathi (soo-JAH-tee). "Jessica and I came from different moms and dads. But we're still sisters — forever."

Laura and Emma were also adopted. "I tell everybody right away, 'This is my sister!'"

"My dad told me that when they were kids, he and my uncle got into fights. But they still liked each other the best," says Will. "They're grown-ups now and they help each other a lot. They let me help, too."

"My mom said she and her sister used to play school all the time. Now it's for real because they're both teachers," says Eddie. "My mom says her sister is more important to her than ever."

"My grandma and my great-aunt have been
sisters for seventy years," says Katherine. "Grandma
says her sister is still her best friend."

Meet the Author and Photographer
Ellen B. Senisi

Ellen Senisi loves to put together words and photos to create books for children. One of the things that most interests her about photography is the fact that although the people or things in a photograph change, the pictures themselves always stay the same.

Look closely at the photographs in *Brothers and Sisters*. You'll see pictures she took several years ago of her three children, Will, Katherine, and Steven.

Other books by Ellen B. Senisi:
For My Family, Love, Allie
Reading Grows

It you'd like to know more about Ellen Senisi and her work as a photographer and author of children's books, visit Education Place.

www.eduplace.com/kids

Think About the Selection

1. Compare two or more of the families in this selection. How are they alike? How are they different?

2. In what ways can an older brother or sister help a younger brother or sister? Give examples from the selection to support your answer.

3. How are brothers and sisters sometimes like best friends?

4. Why is having a brother or sister sometimes hard?

5. **Connecting/Comparing** What have you learned about families from reading this selection?

Creating

Write a Story

Choose a photo from the selection. Write a story about what you think the people in the photo might be thinking or saying.

Tips
- Use a story map to help you get started.
- Think of an interesting title for your story.

Health

Identify Abilities

Choose a photo of a baby, one of someone about your age, and one of a teenager or adult. Write a description of some of the things each person you chose is able to do.

Vocabulary

List Family Words

Work with a partner to make a list of words that name people in a family. Begin with words from the story, such as *brother* and *sister*. Add as many words as you can. Then talk about how the people you named are related to each other.

Bonus Put the words in your list in alphabetical order.

Internet

Solve a Web Hidden Message

Test what you know about brothers and sisters by solving a Web hidden message. You'll find one on Education Place. **www.eduplace.com/kids**

Skill: How to Read a Poem

1. Read the title of the poem.

2. Try to predict what the poem will be about.

3. Read the poem more than once.

4. Compare what you first thought the poem would be about with what you think after reading it again.

Brother and Sister Poems

Do Not Enter

Warning
Do Not Enter
Stop
Wrong Way
Beware
Danger
Do Not Trespass
Caution
Don't You Dare

I taped the signs onto the door —
I thought that's all I'd need.

My brother came in anyway —
He's never learned to read.

by Florence Parry Heide and Roxanne Heide Pierce

I Did Not Eat
Your Ice Cream

I did not eat your ice cream,
I did not swipe your socks.
I did not stuff your lunch box
with rubber bands and rocks.

I did not hide your sweater,
I did not dent your bike,
it must have been my sister,
we look a lot alike.

by Jack Prelutsky

little sister

holds on tight.

My hands hurt

from all that squeezing,

but I don't mind.

She thinks no one will bother her

when I'm around,

and they won't

if I can help it.

And even when I can't,

I try

'cause she believes in me.

by Nikki Grimes

A Personal Narrative

A personal narrative is a true story about something that happened to the writer. Use this student's writing as a model when you write a personal narrative of your own.

My New Kite

A good **beginning** tells what the narrative is about.

One windy day I got a new kite. I had not flown a kite in a long time. My dad took me to a big field to fly it. When we opened the package, a big gust of wind blew the instructions away. My dad had to figure out how to put the kite together. It wasn't easy because the wind kept blowing everything, but we got it put together.

Good writers stay on the **topic**.

Then my dad let me hold the kite in my hand. A huge gust of wind came by. I let go of my kite, held onto the string, and the kite went with the wind way up in the sky. I kept on letting more and more string out until all the string was out. My kite was so high I could hardly see it. I thought that it looked like a tiny dot.

Suddenly, it got close to a tree. I pulled it in the opposite direction. My kite was in trouble. To make matters worse, it started to rain. As I reeled my kite in, it started to pour. I saved my kite just in time.

I can't wait for the next windy day to fly my kite again.

Details help the reader picture what happened.

A good **ending** wraps up the narrative.

Meet the Author

Roy H.
Grade: two
State: Delaware
Hobbies: drawing, riding his bike
What he'd like to be when he grows up: an illustrator

Inside a Bakery

Have you ever stepped inside a **bakery** and smelled fresh bread baking? Have you wondered how bread is made? You'll find out more about what happens in a bakery in the next story. You'll even read two **recipes** for baking.

▼ Bakers prepare their **dough** and bake it early in the day, usually before sunrise, so that **customers** may have the freshest bread possible.

▲ The **ingredients** may change, but the idea is the same: everyone loves a treat from the bakery.

◄ Most **cultures** around the world eat breads or baked goods. Almost all bread recipes use some sort of flour and water. The rest is up to the baker.

Meet the Author
Natasha Wing

Fact File

Favorite Children's Books: *The Polar Express, Charlie and the Chocolate Factory, The Cat in the Hat, The Golden Compass*

Favorite Season: Fall

Favorite Color: Cranberry red

Favorite Cookie: Oatmeal raisin with vanilla chips

Other books by Natasha Wing:

Hippity Hop, Frog on Top
The Night Before Easter

Like Pablo in *Jalapeño Bagels*, Robert Casilla's son, Robert, Jr., speaks both English and Spanish. In fact, Mr. Casilla sometimes uses Robert Jr. as a model for his drawings and illustrations.

Other books illustrated by Robert Casilla:

The Little Painter of Sabana Grande
A Picture Book of Rosa Parks

Meet the Illustrator
Robert Casilla

To find out more about Natasha Wing and Robert Casilla, visit Education Place. **www.eduplace.com/kids**

156

Jalapeño Bagels
by Natasha Wing

illustrated by
Robert Casilla

A boy and his family are getting ready for an important event at school. Read the selection carefully, and think of **questions** to ask about their plans.

"What should I bring to school on Monday for International Day?" I ask my mother. "My teacher told us to bring something from our culture."

"You can bring a treat from the *panadería*," she suggests. Panadería is what Mamá calls our bakery. "Help us bake on Sunday — then you can pick out whatever you want."

"It's a deal," I tell her. I like helping at the bakery. It's warm there, and everything smells so good.

Early Sunday morning, when it is still dark, my mother wakes me up.

"Pablo, it's time to go to work," she says.

We walk down the street to the bakery. My father turns on the lights. My mother turns on the ovens. She gets out the pans and ingredients for *pan dulce* (pahn DOOL-seh). Pan dulce is Mexican sweet bread.

I help my mother mix and knead the dough. She shapes rolls and loaves of bread and slides them into the oven. People tell her she makes the best pan dulce in town.

"Maybe I'll bring pan dulce to school," I tell her.

Next we make *empanadas de calabaza* — pumpkin
turnovers. I'm in charge of spooning the pumpkin filling.
Mamá folds the dough in half and presses the edges with
a fork. She bakes them until they are flaky and golden
brown. Some customers come to our bakery just for
her turnovers.

"Maybe I'll bring empanadas de calabaza instead."

"You'll figure it out," she says. "Ready to make *chango* bars?"

Mamá lets me pour in the chocolate chips and nuts. When she's not looking, I pour in more chocolate chips.

"I could bring chango bars. They're my favorite dessert."

"Mine, too" says Mamá. "This batch should be especially good. I put in extra chips."

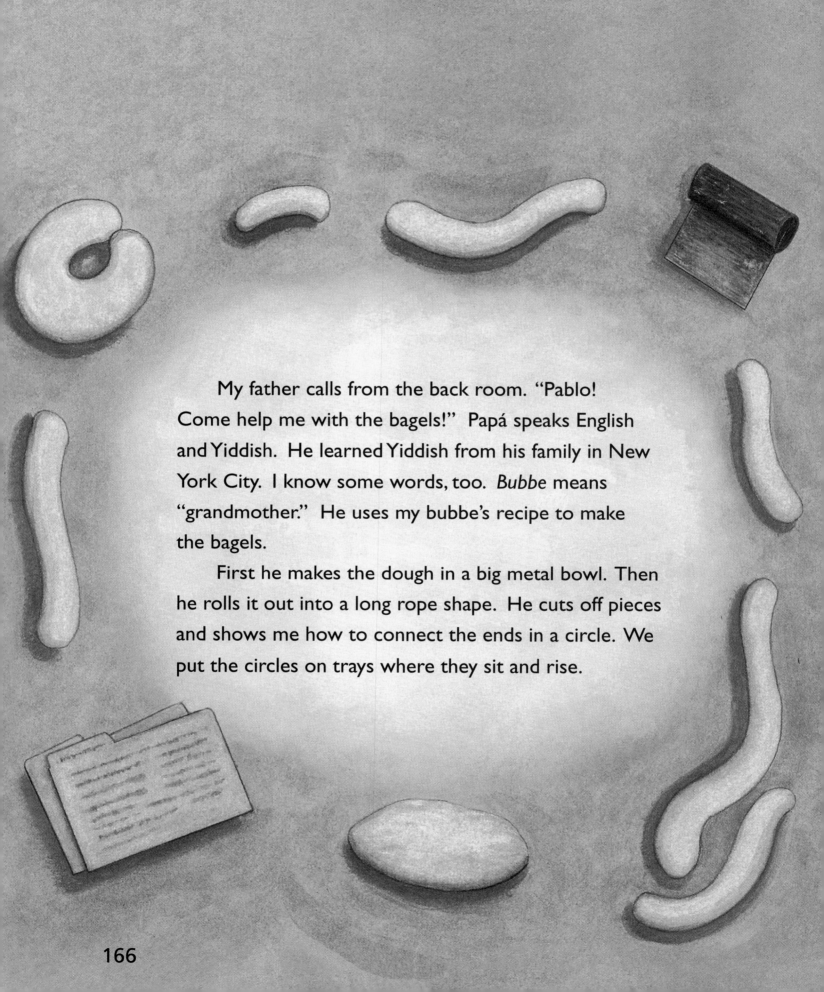

My father calls from the back room. "Pablo! Come help me with the bagels!" Papá speaks English and Yiddish. He learned Yiddish from his family in New York City. I know some words, too. *Bubbe* means "grandmother." He uses my bubbe's recipe to make the bagels.

First he makes the dough in a big metal bowl. Then he rolls it out into a long rope shape. He cuts off pieces and shows me how to connect the ends in a circle. We put the circles on trays where they sit and rise.

While we are waiting my father makes *challah*, Jewish braided bread. He lets me practice braiding challah dough at my own counter. It's a lot like braiding hair. The customers say it is almost too beautiful to eat.

"Maybe I'll bring a loaf of challah to school," I tell Papá. He smiles.

When the bagel dough has risen, he boils the bagels in a huge pot of water and fishes them out with a long slotted spoon. I sprinkle on poppy seeds and sesame seeds, and then they go in the oven.

"Maybe I could bring sesame-seed bagels with cream cheese."

"No *lox?*" Lox is smoked salmon. My father's favorite bagel is pumpernickel with a smear of cream cheese and lox.

I crinkle my nose. "Lox tastes like fish. Jam is better."

My mother joins us and helps my father make another batch of bagels — *jalapeño* (ha-la-PEN-yo) bagels. My parents use their own special recipe. While Papá kneads the dough, Mamá chops the jalapeño *chiles*. She tosses them into the dough and adds dried red peppers. We roll, cut, make circles, and let them rise. I can't wait until they are done because I am getting hungry.

"Have you decided what you're going to bring to school?" asks Mamá.

"It's hard to choose. Everything is so good," I tell her. I look at Papá. "Except for lox."

"You should decide before we open," warns Mamá,
"or else our customers will buy everything up."

I walk past all the sweet breads, chango bars,
and bagels.

I think about my mother and my father and all the
different things they make in the bakery.

And suddenly I know exactly what I'm going to bring.

"Jalapeño bagels," I tell my parents. "And I'll spread them with cream cheese and jam."

"Why jalapeño bagels?" asks Papá.

"Because they are a mixture of both of you. Just like me!"

These recipes are from a real Mexican-Jewish-American bakery, Los Bagels Bakery & Cafe, in Arcata, California. Kids should ask grown-ups for help with both recipes.

Chango Bars

$\frac{1}{2}$ cup butter

$\frac{1}{2}$ cup margarine

2 cups brown sugar

3 eggs

$2\frac{1}{3}$ cups flour

1 tablespoon baking powder

1 teaspoon salt

1 cup chocolate chips

1 cup mixed nuts

Melt butter and margarine. While this is melting, cream brown sugar and eggs, then add melted butter and margarine. Combine flour, baking powder, and salt and stir into sugar mixture. Fold in chocolate chips and nuts. Pour mixture into greased 9 inch x 13 inch baking pan and bake 45 to 50 minutes at 350 degrees.

For this recipe you will need lots of time. But these bagels are worth the wait!

Jalapeño Bagels

$1\frac{3}{4}$ cups lukewarm water

$\frac{1}{2}$ teaspoon dry yeast

2 teaspoons salt

$1\frac{1}{2}$ tablespoons sugar

5 to 6 cups flour

$\frac{1}{3}$ cup jalapeños, chopped

$\frac{1}{4}$ cup dried red peppers

Mix water, yeast, salt, and sugar. Add flour and jalapeños and mix into a ball. Knead for 10 to 12 minutes, adding more flour if necessary, until dough is stiff. Add red peppers and knead for 3 minutes. Let dough rest 10 minutes, then cut into 12 pieces with a knife.

Roll each piece of dough on a table to form long tube-like shapes. Then, for each of the twelve pieces, connect the two ends by overlapping them about $\frac{3}{4}$ of an inch and rolling the ends together to make a ring shape. Make sure each joint is secure or it will come apart while boiling.

Cover with a damp towel and let rise 1 to $1\frac{1}{2}$ hours in a warm spot. In a large pot, bring 1 to 2 gallons of water to a rolling boil. Place bagels in boiling water and boil until they float (15 to 30 seconds). Remove with a slotted spoon and place on a lightly greased cookie sheet. Bake at **400** degrees for 10 to 15 minutes or until golden brown.

Responding

Think About the Selection

1. Why are jalapeño bagels a good choice of food for Pablo to take to school for International Day?

2. What do you think might be fun about having a family business? What might be difficult?

3. Which of the foods described in the story do you think you'd like best? Why?

4. Pablo is helpful in several ways at the panadería. In what ways can you be helpful at home or in your classroom?

5. **Connecting/Comparing** If Pablo had a younger brother or sister, what might he tell him or her about their family?

Explaining

Write a How-to Paragraph

Think of a food you know how to make. Write a paragraph that explains how to make it. Begin by telling what you are going to make. Then tell step-by-step how to make it.

Tips

- Start by making a list of ingredients.
- Use time-order words such as *first, next,* and *then.*

Math

Compare Measurements

Look at the recipes for chango bars and jalapeño bagels on pages 175–177. Then answer these questions.

- Which recipe uses more flour?

- Which recipe uses more salt? How much more?

- Which recipe uses more sugar?

Bonus Write two more questions about the recipes. Ask a classmate to answer them.

Social Studies

Make an International Day Poster

Plan your own school or classroom International Day with a small group. Think of favorite family foods. Then make a poster to advertise International Day. Include the foods you chose on your poster.

Solve a Web Word Scramble

Learn more about baking and bakeries when you solve a Web word scramble on Education Place.

www.eduplace.com/kids

Skill: Adjust Your Rate of Reading

❶ Ask yourself what you already know or would like to learn about the topic.

❷ When you read for information, slow down your reading to make sure that you understand the facts.

❸ When you come to a part that is easy to understand, read at your normal pace.

Welcome to the Kitchen

by Carolyn E. Moore, Mimi Kerr, and Robert Shulman

The kitchen is the best place to be when it comes to good food. The cooking is fun and so is the eating. You can make snacks, meals, special holiday treats for yourself and for your whole family.

If you haven't done much cooking before, you should have an adult with you who can show you how to use kitchen equipment.

Safety First

1. Dress safely. Roll up long sleeves and pull your hair back so nothing gets into the food that doesn't belong there. Wear an apron so food doesn't get where it doesn't belong.

2. Keep your fingers away from the sharp edge of a knife. Pick knives up by the handle, not by the blade. Always cut food on a cutting board, not while holding food in your hand.

3. Make sure electric appliances are turned off before you plug them in.

4. Use pot holders or hot pads when you pick up pots from the stove or put things in or take things out of the oven.

5. Don't let the handles of pots stick out over the side of the stove where someone could bump into them.

6. Turn the oven or stove burner off as soon as you have finished with it.

Have you ever grumbled at someone, even though you weren't really mad at them? Or have you fussed and argued when you were tired, or groaned when you broke a favorite toy? Everyone has bad days now and then.

People sometimes get angry, or act grumpily, when they're having a bad day. In the story you are about to read, a girl is upset when someone can't do what he promised he would do. Find out what lessons she learns from her own bad day.

Meet the Author and Illustrator
Pat Cummings

Fact File

Birthday: November 9

Favorite children's books:
The Chronicles of Narnia
by C.S. Lewis

How she makes her art:
She has used all kinds of
materials to make her books,
including watercolors, acrylics,
wallpaper, and rubber stamps.

Her favorite illustrators:
Lane Smith, Chris Van
Allsburg, Floyd Cooper,
and Lois Ehlert

Pets: She has a cat
named Cash.

Other Books:

*Petey Moroni's Camp
    Runamok Diary*

Clean Your Room, Harvey Moon

Storm in the Night

Internet

It you liked reading *Carousel*, and want to read
more about Pat Cummings, visit our Web site.

www.eduplace.com/kids

184

CAROUSEL

BY PAT CUMMINGS

Strategy Focus

A little girl's birthday turns into a bad day. As you read the story, try to **predict** how it will end.

185

Alex didn't want her hair braided or her shiny
shoes buckled or every single little pearly button
buttoned on her dress. And she definitely didn't want
her birthday cake after dinner with just her aunts.

"Where's Daddy?" she grumbled for the eighth time. "Hold still, Alex," sighed her mother, tugging away. Off went the sneakers. On went the bows. Off went the jeans. On came the frills.

Dinner lasted forever. Alex pushed peas from side
to side on her plate. She stabbed a potato chunk with
her fork, dragged it through the gravy, and ate it like an
ice-cream cone.

"Alex," her mother warned, and then smiled at the
aunts. "Let's open your presents before we cut the cake."

Before Alex could say, "Let's wait for Daddy," her aunts had whisked away the dinner dishes, pulled balloons out of bags, and popped party hats on everyone's heads. There was a pile of presents to open.

Alex opened Auntie Lea's gift first. "I have a *million* pairs of pajamas," she mumbled grumpily.

She unwrapped a frothy ballerina tutu from Aunt Ruby. Aunt Ruby liked things to sparkle. "Looks scratchy," Alex fussed under her breath. Her mother made a face at her, but Alex didn't care.

Then, burrowing through puffs of tissues, Alex found a pair of long, fuzzy, hot pink slipper-socks. They had rabbit ears and googly eyes and WHISKERS! Aunt Rose scurried to grab her camera.

"No way," Alex groaned.

"Alex!" her mother said sharply. "Maybe you need to go to bed." Alex quickly hugged her aunts and thanked them. She wasn't mad at *them*. "But Daddy promised . . ." she began.

"He said he'd try, honey. And," her mother added, handing her the last gift, "he said to give you this just in case he didn't get back from his trip in time."

Alex felt her cheeks getting hot. *He knew he
wouldn't be home!* She tugged at the paper and yanked
off the ribbons.

"Oooooooohhh . . . aaaaaahhhh!" the aunts cried.
There before her was the most perfect little carousel
that Alex had ever seen.

"He said he'd be here!" Alex hissed angrily. The aunts stopped ooooohing. "He promised!" She kicked away the ribbons at her feet.

"That's it, young lady! No cake for you. Say good-night." Her mother wasn't smiling.

But Alex didn't care. She wanted to blow the candy roses right off the cake anyway. "Good-NIGHT!" Alex barked. She marched upstairs holding the carousel by one of its delicate little poles.

"I don't care." Alex twisted the bows out of her hair and pulled off her party dress without stopping to undo a single little button. "He knew it. He knew it," she fussed at the little animals.

Alex heard her aunts laughing downstairs. "They're eating up my cake!"

She jumped into bed, kicked the blankets back,
and sent the carousel tumbling. There was a soft snap.
Slowly, she picked up the carousel and studied it. The
tiny zebra looked wobbly. With just a wiggle, it broke
off completely!

Its little painted face looked almost angry. She had to fix the carousel before her father came home, or he would think she didn't like her gift. She yawned. She turned. There would be time in the morning. . . .

Alex didn't remember falling asleep. Something tickled her knee, waking her in time to see the last of the carousel animals hopping lightly out of her window.

"Oh, no," she gasped. They had to come back. The empty carousel was on its side, all deserted and sad-looking. "Daddy," she whispered.

Alex ran to the window, and, knowing what she had to do, slipped easily down into the soft grass outside.

The animals were getting away! Alex took off running. Even as she hurried after them, it seemed that the moonlight was making them grow, their legs stretching farther and farther. A paw here, ears there, whiskers in and out of the blue nighttime leaves.

And just when she
thought she had lost them forever,
Alex saw them waiting beyond the tall trees.
They were waiting for her.

Alex tiptoed up to the zebra. She carefully
climbed up on his back. A little bit of pole was
sticking up just where she had broken it off.

"Sorry," she whispered in his ear. Had he
heard her?

The zebra shook his mane and
began to trot. Then he galloped,
then he flew.

Around
and around and
around, all of the animals were
running with him. From frog to
flamingo, from rabbit to giraffe, Alex
took turns: upside down, right
side up, one hand, no hands,
both eyes closed.

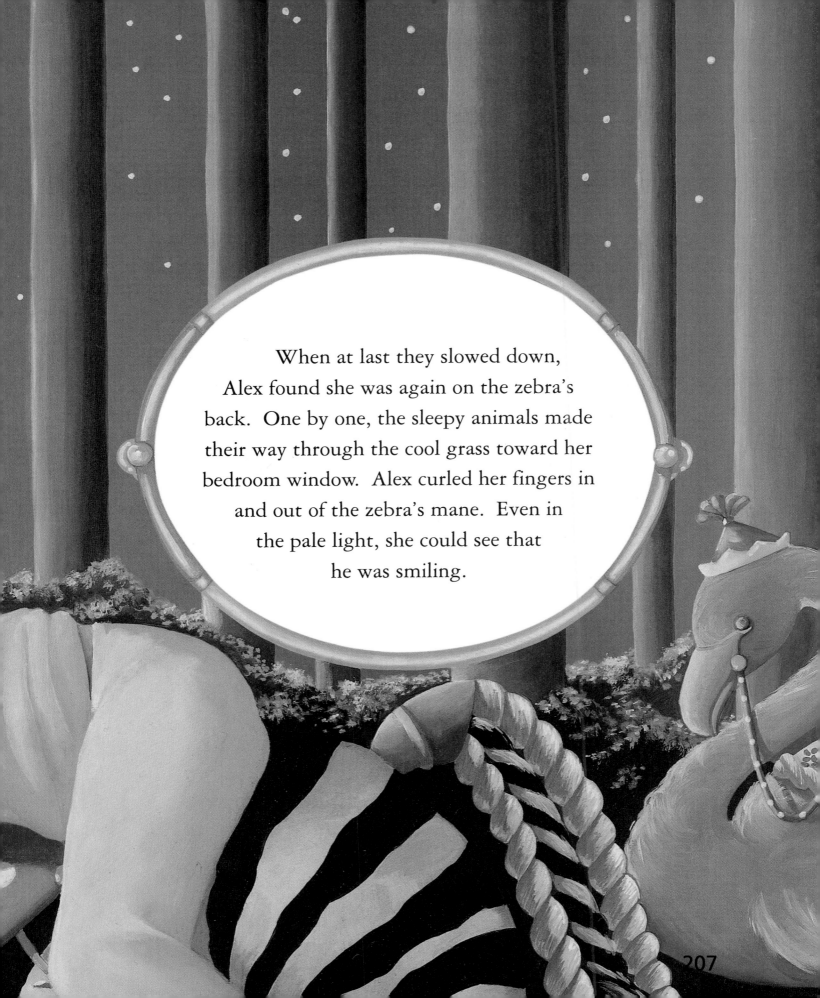

When at last they slowed down, Alex found she was again on the zebra's back. One by one, the sleepy animals made their way through the cool grass toward her bedroom window. Alex curled her fingers in and out of the zebra's mane. Even in the pale light, she could see that he was smiling.

One eye opened. Then the other. It was morning.

"Oh, dear!" Alex sat straight up. She remembered everything. She remembered the carousel animals had all gotten loose.

She pulled the covers apart, but now there wasn't a single little animal in sight. She rolled onto the floor and peered under the bed. No flamingo. No leopard. Nothing!

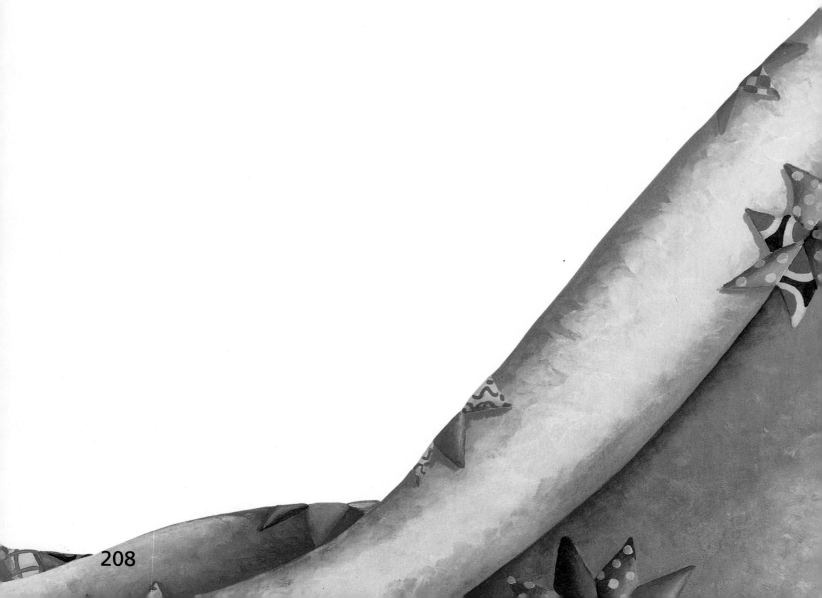

"Happy birthday, sleepyhead. You awake?" Her father was home! Hugging Alex, he kissed her smack on the nose. Then he saw the carousel sitting underneath the window.

"Daddy, I'm sorry I broke it," Alex said.

"And I'm sorry I missed your birthday," her father answered. "I got really angry when my plane was so late in coming home. But I couldn't stay angry. Know why?"

Alex shook her head.

"Because the same thing that made me angry made me happy when I thought about it. I was happy just to be coming home."

"Breakfast, anyone?" her mother asked, going straight to the window to close it. "It got a bit windy in here last night." She winked at Alex.

Alex kissed them both.

"We have a little work to do," her dad said, pressing the tiny zebra into Alex's hand. "What's for breakfast?"

"Oh, scrambled cake and ice-cream omelettes." Her mother laughed and headed downstairs.

Alex took her dad by the hand.

"And put on those cute little slippers for Daddy, Alex!" her mother called out.

Alex squeezed her dad's hand. He was going to *love* those slippers!

Responding

Think About the Selection

1. How do you think Alex felt about her behavior the day after her party?

2. How do you think Alex's dad felt about missing her birthday party?

3. What do you think happened to Alex between the time she went to bed and the time she woke up in the morning?

4. How might you feel if you broke a special gift that you liked very much?

5. **Connecting/Comparing** Compare Pablo in *Jalapeño Bagels* to Alex. In what ways are they alike? How are they different?

Write a Personal Narrative

Alex's father gave her a very special gift. Think of a gift that you've given or received. Compare your memorable gift to Alex's carousel. Write a story about your gift.

- Make sure the events in your story are in order.
- Write the word *I* with a capital letter.

216

Art

Design a Carousel Animal

Choose an animal from the story, or think of a favorite animal. Use crayons or markers to draw and color your animal. With a group, make a carousel from cut paper, and place your animals on your carousel.

Listening and Speaking

Practice Politeness

Alex did not thank her aunts properly for their gifts. Take turns with a classmate. Role-play Alex thanking her aunt. Tell about the gift and explain why you enjoyed it.

Internet

Build a Story

Do you think you know the story inside-out and backwards? Test your knowledge of *Carousel*. Visit Education Place and unscramble our mixed-up story.

www.eduplace.com/kids

Carousel
Designed by Kids

by Kathy Kranking, from *Ranger Rick* magazine

Have you ever drawn a picture of your favorite animal? Imagine if someone built an exact copy of your drawing — and made it big enough for you to ride. That's what happened to the drawings of a bunch of lucky kids in New York City. And now the kids can ride their animals any time they want!

The animals are all part of the Totally Kid Carousel in New York's Riverbank State Park. It's the first carousel in the world designed by kids.

So how did it all come about? The wizard behind this magical idea is an artist named Milo Mottola. The city officials wanted an artist to build a carousel in the park. They asked Milo to come up with ideas.

Milo thought for a long time. Then he saw a young friend draw a horse. "That's it!" Milo said. "I could ask kids to draw funny, lumpy carousel animals. They would be charming and wonderful too!"

So Milo talked to lots and lots of kids in the neighborhood around Riverbank State Park. Most were first and second graders. He got them to make drawings of their favorite animals.

Then Milo had a hard job to do. Only 36 animals would fit on the carousel. So he had to pick from a thousand drawings the kids had done. Finally the choices were made.

How did each animal go from a drawing to a carousel critter? Here's what happened with this deer, drawn by Edwin Vargas.

How they're made

Lizzie Queena Castle shows off her carousel horse. See how much it looks like her drawing? The carousel animals show what happens when you take a good idea — and give it a whirl!

221

Thunder and Lightning

You have probably heard **thunder** as it **rumbled** during a storm. Thunder is the loud noise that you hear after you see a flash of **lightning**.

Lightning is a quick flash or **bolt** of electricity that lights up the sky during a thunderstorm. Thunderstorms often happen when the **weather** is warm.

In the story you are about to read, a grandmother helps a little girl get over her fear of thunderstorms.

The next time you see a thunderstorm on the **horizon**, you can stay safe if you remain inside your house or in a car.

Meet the
Author and Illustrator
Patricia Polacco

Storytelling has always been a favorite tradition in Patricia Polacco's family. So it's only natural that she would become a great storyteller herself. *Thunder Cake* is a story based on Ms. Polacco's memories of life on her grandmother's farm in Michigan.

Patricia Polacco writes her stories in her house, which she named "Meteor Ridge." Her art supplies won't all fit in her home office, so she has a studio in another house a block away, just for illustrating!

Other books by Patricia Polacco:

My Rotten Redheaded Older Brother
Rechenka's Eggs
Meteor!

Patricia Polacco spends a lot of time in her studio, working on her books. To find out how she makes her illustrations, visit Education Place. **www.eduplace.com/kids**

thunder cake

PATRICIA POLACCO

Strategy Focus

While you read about a young girl's fear of
thunderstorms, **monitor** your understanding.
If you have questions, stop and reread to **clarify**.

225

Grandma looked at the horizon, drew a deep breath and said, "This is Thunder Cake baking weather, all right. Looks like a storm coming to me."

"Child, you come out from under that bed. It's only thunder you're hearing," my grandma said.

The air was hot, heavy, and damp. A loud clap of thunder shook the house, rattled the windows, and made me grab her close.

"Steady, child," she cooed. "Unless you let go of me, we won't be able to make a Thunder Cake today!"

"Thunder Cake?" I stammered as I hugged her even closer.

"Don't pay attention to that old thunder, except to see how close the storm is getting. When you see the lightning, start counting . . . real slow. When you hear the thunder, stop counting. That number is how many miles away the storm is. Understand?" she asked. "We need to know how far away the storm is, so we have time to make the cake and get it into the oven before the storm comes, or it won't be real Thunder Cake."

Her eyes surveyed the black clouds a way off in the distance. Then she strode into the kitchen. Her worn hands pulled a thick book from the shelf above the woodstove.

"Let's find that recipe, child," she crowed as she lovingly fingered the grease-stained pages to a creased spot.

"Here it is . . . Thunder Cake!"

She carefully penned the ingredients on a piece of notepaper. "Now let's gather all the things we'll need!" she exclaimed as she scurried toward the back door.

We were by the barn door when a huge bolt of lightning flashed. I started counting, like Grandma told me to, "1–2–3–4–5–6–7–8–9–10."

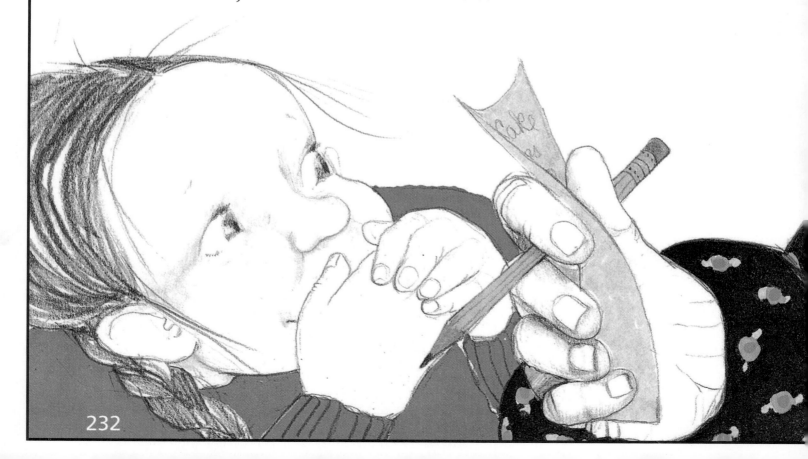

Then the thunder ROARED!

"Ten miles . . . it's ten miles away," Grandma said as she looked at the sky. "About an hour away, I'd say. You'll have to hurry, child. Gather them eggs careful-like," she said.

Eggs from mean old Nellie Peck hen. I was scared. I knew she would try to peck me.

"I'm here, she won't hurt you. Just get them eggs," Grandma said softly.

The lightning flashed again.

"1–2–3–4–5–6–7–8–9" I counted.

"Nine miles," Grandma reminded me.

Milk was next. Milk from old Kick Cow. As Grandma milked her, Kick Cow turned and looked mean, right at me. I was scared. She looked so big.

ZIP went the lightning. "1–2–3–4–5–6–7–8" I counted.

BAROOOOOOOOM went the thunder.

"Eight miles, child," Grandma croaked. "Now we have to get chocolate and sugar and flour from the dry shed."

I was scared as we walked down the path from the farmhouse through Tangleweed Woods to the dry shed. Suddenly the lightning slit the sky!

"1–2–3–4–5–6–7" I counted.

BOOOOOOM BA-BOOOOOOM, crashed the thunder. It scared me a lot, but I kept walking with Grandma.

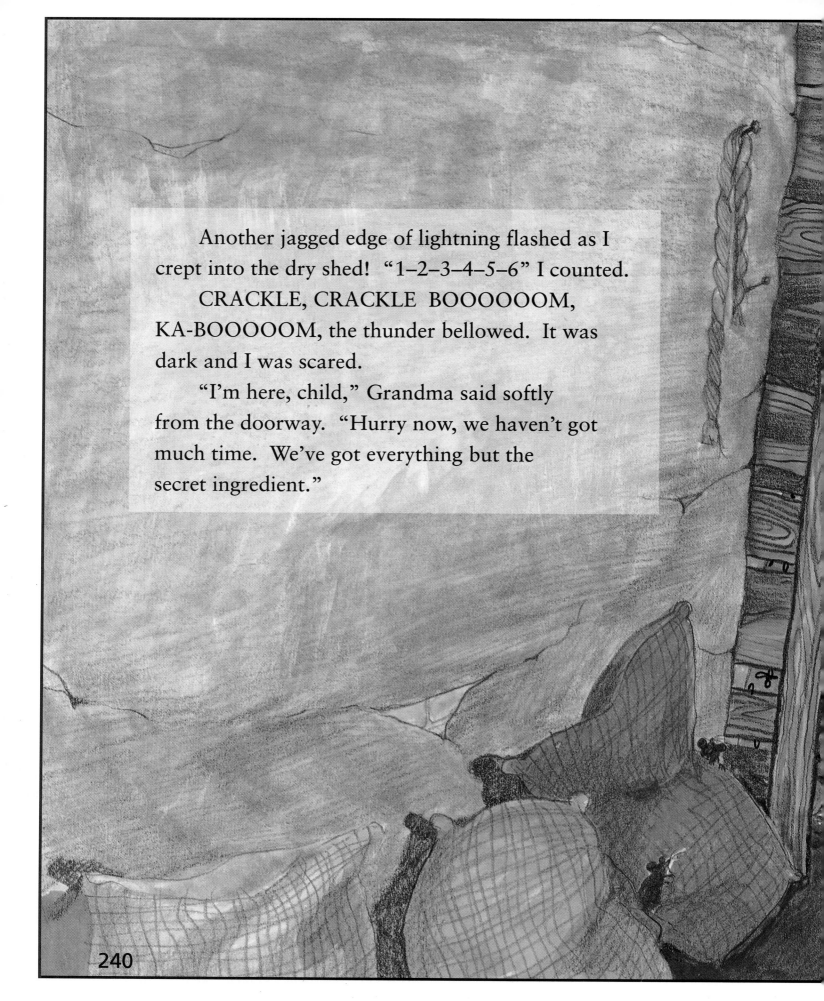

Another jagged edge of lightning flashed as I crept into the dry shed! "1–2–3–4–5–6" I counted.

CRACKLE, CRACKLE BOOOOOOM, KA-BOOOOOM, the thunder bellowed. It was dark and I was scared.

"I'm here, child," Grandma said softly from the doorway. "Hurry now, we haven't got much time. We've got everything but the secret ingredient."

241

"Three overripe tomatoes and some strawberries," Grandma whispered as she squinted at the list.

I climbed up high on the trellis. The ground looked a long way down. I was scared.

"I'm here, child," she said. Her voice was steady and soft. "You won't fall."

I reached three luscious tomatoes while she picked strawberries. Lightning again!

"1–2–3–4–5" I counted.

KA-BANG BOOOOOOOOAROOOOM, the thunder growled.

We hurried back to the house and the warm kitchen, and we measured the ingredients. I poured them into the mixing bowl while Grandma mixed. I churned butter for the frosting and melted chocolate. Finally, we poured the batter into the cake pans and put them into the oven together.

Lightning lit the kitchen! I only counted to three and the thunder RRRRUMBLED and CRASHED.

"Three miles away," Grandma said, "and the cake is in the oven. We made it! We'll have a real Thunder Cake!"

As we waited for the cake, Grandma looked out the window for a long time. "Why, you aren't afraid of thunder. You're too brave!" she said as she looked right at me.

"I'm not brave, Grandma," I said. "I was under the bed! Remember?"

"But you got out from under it," she answered, "and you got eggs from mean old Nellie Peck Hen, you got milk from old Kick Cow, you went through Tangleweed Woods to the dry shed, you climbed the trellis in the barnyard. From where I sit, only a very brave person could have done all them things!"

I thought and thought as the storm rumbled closer. She was right. I was brave!

"Brave people can't be afraid of a sound, child," she said as we spread out the tablecloth and set the table. When we were done, we hurried into the kitchen to take the cake out of the oven. After the cake had cooled, we frosted it.

Just then the lightning flashed, and this time it lit the whole sky.

Even before the last flash had faded, the thunder ROLLED, BOOOOMED, CRASHED, and BBBBAAAAARRRROOOOOOOMMMMMMMMMMED just above us. The storm was here!

"Perfect," Grandma cooed, "just perfect." She beamed as she added the last strawberry to the glistening chocolate frosting on top of our Thunder Cake.

As rain poured down on our roof, Grandma cut a wedge for each of us. She poured us steaming cups of tea from the samovar.

When the thunder ROARED above us so hard it shook the windows and rattled the dishes in the cupboards, we just smiled and ate our Thunder Cake.

From that time on, I never feared the voice of thunder again.

My Grandma's Thunder Cake

Cream together, one at a time

1 cup shortening

$1\frac{3}{4}$ cup sugar

1 teaspoon vanilla

3 eggs, separated

(Blend yolks in. Beat whites
until they are stiff, then fold in.)

1 cup cold water

$\frac{1}{3}$ cup pureed tomatoes

Sift together

$2\frac{1}{2}$ cups cake flour

$\frac{1}{2}$ cup dry cocoa

$1\frac{1}{2}$ teaspoons baking soda

1 teaspoon salt

Mix dry mixture into creamy mixture.

Bake in two greased and floured $8\frac{1}{2}$-inch round pans
at 350° for 35 to 40 minutes.

Frost with chocolate butter frosting. Top with strawberries.

Responding

Think About the Selection

1. Why do you suppose Grandma wants the little girl to go outside?

2. How do you think Grandma learned not to be afraid during a thunderstorm?

3. What does the author do to make you feel that a storm is coming?

4. Why do you think Patricia Polacco decided to share this story?

5. **Connecting/Comparing** How is food important in *Jalapeño Bagels* and *Thunder Cake*?

 Creating

Write an Acrostic Poem

Choose a storm word from the story. Write the word down the left-hand side of a piece of paper. Use the letters of the word you chose to begin the first word of each line of your poem.

Tips

- Make a list of words that begin with each letter to help you get started.
- Your poem does not need to rhyme.

256

Compare Temperatures

Place a thermometer outside on asphalt in a sunny place. Wait three minutes, then record the temperature. Next, place the thermometer on grass. Record the temperature after three minutes. Compare the temperatures.

 Tips

- Use a T-chart to record your information.
- Use a timer to keep track of the time.

Identify Feelings

How does the girl feel about thunder when the story begins? Find a picture that shows that feeling. Then find another picture that shows how she feels later. With a partner, talk about details that make the two pictures different.

Internet

Complete a Web Word Jumble

All of the thunder cake ingredients are mixed up! Visit Education Place to solve this scrambled puzzle.

www.eduplace.com/kids

257

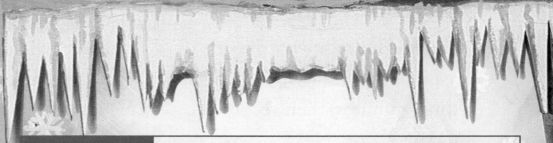

Sun and Ice

From *Out of the Bag: The Paper Bag Players Book of Plays*

Skill: How to Read a Play

❶ Predict what the play is about by reading the title.

❷ As you read, scan the **cast** of **characters.** This tells you who is in the play.

❸ Pay attention to the **stage directions.** These directions tell you what to do and when to do it.

❹ Take turns reading each character's lines aloud. Plays are meant to be performed and should be practiced aloud.

Characters: Girl (Narrator), **Sun, Ice, Seed, Cloud**

Girl: Winter, spring, summer, fall. Winter, spring, summer, fall.

Ice: *(Enters)* Not this year.

Girl: This year winter refused to leave. *(Exits)*

Ice: Why should it? The whole world is cold and white and beautiful. Lakes are frozen. Mountains are covered with snow. Icicles hang from the trees. Winter is the most powerful force on Earth.

Sun: *(Enters)* With one exception.

Ice: It's the sun! He's going to ruin everything.

Sun: You've made everything cold, hard, and still — but I'm going to warm things up, make them move and grow. *(As they argue, Ice tries to cover Sun, and Sun tries to cover Ice.)*

Ice: I make snow and blizzards.

Sun: I make it hot.

Ice: I make it cold.

Sun: Hot.

Ice: Cold. *(Sound of thunder from offstage)*

Sun: Thunder! *(Cloud enters.)*

Seed: *(Enters)* Where, where, where can I find a spot to plant myself?

Sun: What is it?

Cloud: It's a seed.

Seed: I'm looking for a place to get started, but the ground is so cold and hard! Sun, can't you warm things up — just a bit?

259

Sun: (*Moving close to Cloud*) Excuse me, Cloud, this little seed needs me.

Seed: (*To Sun*) What's Ice doing here? He shouldn't be here.

Sun: You heard her, Ice. It's time for you to go. (*Now Sun feels very powerful and chases Ice around the stage.*)

Sun: Melt!

Ice: I'm going, but I'll be back. (*Exits*)

Sun: (*To Seed*) Now you can start growing.

Seed: Just in time. My roots are itching and my leaves are ready to pop. I've got to grow, I just can't stop. I need some sun.

Sun: The sun is here. (*Makes a circular movement around Seed, suggesting sun rays*) How's that?

Seed: I feel dry.

Cloud: You need rain.

Sun: *(Circling Seed)* Sun.

Cloud: Rain.

Sun: How's that feel?

Seed: That feels just right.

Sun: I think it's time. Come on,
little seed, you can do it.
Come on, you're almost there.
Come on. *(Flower is fully opened.)*
Well done, little flower!

Cloud: Oh, little flower, you look
pretty good. I'm done in.
I'm all wiped out.
(Exits with a heavy, weary walk)

Sun: The seed has become a flower,
and it's a beautiful day.

The End

✔ Writing an Answer to a Question

Many tests ask you to write an answer to a question about something you have read. You may need to write one or two sentences for the answer. Here is a sample test question for *Brothers and Sisters*. Use the tips to help you answer this kind of test question.

Tips

- Read the directions and the question carefully so you know what to do.
- Make sure you know what the question is asking.
- Think about your answer before you write.

Write your answer to this question.

1 In what two ways is having a sister like having a brother?

_____

_____

_____

_____

Now read one student's answer and see how he planned it.

When you have a sister or brother it's

important to learn to share. Also, a younger

sister or brother doesn't always play games

the way you're supposed to.

This answer is good because it tells two ways that having a sister can be like having a brother.

I can think of one way that having a sister can be like having a brother, but the question asks for two ways. I'll look at the selection again for more information.

Now I know two ways that having a sister or brother can be the same. I'll write my answer.

Biography

Would you enjoy getting to know someone new today? If so, read a biography!

What is a biography?
- It is a true story about someone's life.
- It gives facts about what the person did.
- It tells about events that happened during the person's life.

Contents

REACH FOR THE STARS

The Ellen Ochoa Story

BY ELENA ALONSO

It was April 17, 1993. The space shuttle *Discovery* was about to return to Earth after more than nine days in space. One of the five astronauts on board, Dr. Ellen Ochoa, had just made history. Dr. Ochoa had become the first Hispanic woman to travel in space.

Discovery **lifts off.**

Ellen Ochoa was born in 1958 in Los Angeles, California. She was eleven years old when astronauts walked on the moon for the first time. She didn't dream then that some day she too would become an astronaut.

The crew of
Discovery

"At that time, there weren't any women astronauts and also very few who were scientists," she says. "So it didn't occur to me when I was in school that this was something I could grow up and do."

Today, Ellen enjoys speaking to children about her work as an astronaut. She encourages children, especially girls, to study math and science.

Ellen's favorite subjects in school were math and music. She also played the flute. In fact, she became so good at it that she was asked to play with a youth orchestra in San Diego.

The space shuttle's
cargo bay

"Only you put limitations on yourself about what you can achieve, so don't be afraid to reach for the stars."

Several years after college, Ellen decided that she really wanted to learn how to be an astronaut. She moved to Houston, Texas, where the NASA space program is located. Meanwhile, she took up a new hobby: she learned how to fly an airplane!

In 1990, NASA picked Ellen for its astronaut program. Three years later, she made her first space shuttle flight. Her job was to work a robotic arm that can send small satellites into space and then catch them again.

Ellen Ochoa with her son

Ellen Ochoa flew with five other astronauts on the *Discovery* in 1999.

Since her first flight, Ellen has spent almost 500 hours in space. On one trip, Ellen and her team traveled 4 million miles in 235 hours and 13 minutes!

Ellen is proud to be the first Hispanic female astronaut. She tells children to work hard to become whatever they want to be. She says, "Only you put limitations on yourself about what you can achieve, so don't be afraid to reach for the stars."

PRESIDENT
Theodore Roosevelt

by Stephen Berman

BEING PRESIDENT OF THE UNITED STATES is something that many people only dream about. But Theodore Roosevelt did more than dream about it. "Keep your eyes on the stars, and your feet on the ground," he loved to say.

President Roosevelt

President Roosevelt and his family

TR, as his friends called him, was born in 1858 in New York City. When he was very young, he was sick with asthma. Later, he started exercising every day. He became strong and fit. He learned to love sports and the outdoors.

TR loved to read and write too. Most of all, he loved nature. When he was seven years old, he started the Roosevelt Museum of Natural History in his family's house. It was filled with bones and skins and skulls of animals he had found. His love of nature remained an important part of his life when he was president.

An image of Theodore Roosevelt's face is carved in stone, sixty feet high, at Mount Rushmore in South Dakota.

Theodore Roosevelt was elected vice president in 1900. When President William McKinley was killed less than a year later, TR became president. He was only forty-two years old, the youngest president ever.

Theodore Roosevelt and a friend look out on Yosemite National Park.

While TR was president, he made laws to create national forests and national parks. That's how he became known as the "Conservation President."

Theodore Roosevelt was president from 1901 to 1909. He died ten years later on January 16, 1919. He was sixty years old.

Today we can still enjoy the beautiful parks he helped create.

Theodore Roosevelt National Park, North Dakota

TR and the Teddy Bear

DID YOU KNOW THAT teddy bears are named after President Theodore Roosevelt? Some toy makers had the idea of making stuffed toy bears. They knew that President Roosevelt was interested in animals, so one of the toy makers asked for his permission to call them Teddy's bears. TR liked the bears, but he never did like the nickname "Teddy."

WILMA RUDOLPH

OLYMPIC TRACK CHAMPION

BY VERONICA FREEMAN ELLIS

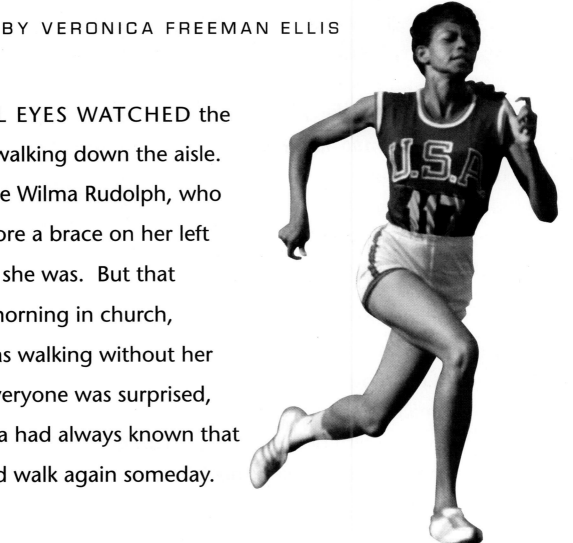

ALL EYES WATCHED the little girl walking down the aisle. Wasn't she Wilma Rudolph, who always wore a brace on her left leg? Yes, she was. But that Sunday morning in church, Wilma was walking without her brace. Everyone was surprised, but Wilma had always known that she would walk again someday.

Wilma wins the 100–meter dash.

Wilma runs a 400-meter relay.

"The doctors told me I would never walk," said Wilma many years later, "but my mother told me I would, so I believed my mother."

Wilma Rudolph was born in Bethlehem, Tennessee, in 1940. Just before her fifth birthday, Wilma became very ill. Her illness caused her to lose the use of her left leg.

Wilma receives one of her three gold medals.

Wilma was determined to walk. She did exercises every day to make her leg stronger. Even though doctors had put a steel brace on her leg, Wilma practiced walking every day without it. When she was twelve years old, she took off her brace for good.

At sixteen, Wilma Rudolph became the youngest member of the 1956 U.S. Olympic track team. That year she won a bronze medal in the relay race.

In 1960, Wilma became world famous. At the Olympics in Rome, Italy, she won a gold medal for the 100-meter dash. She won a second gold medal for the 200-meter dash.

It was time for the 400-meter relay race. Wilma was the final runner on her team. It was up to her to cross the finish line. When her teammate handed her the baton, Wilma nearly dropped it! Her team fell to third place, but Wilma didn't give up. She ran as hard as she could — and she won.

IMPORTANT DATES AND EVENTS

1940

Wilma Rudolph is born on June 23.

1956

She wins a bronze medal at the Olympics.

1960

She wins three gold medals at the Rome Olympics.

Wilma Rudolph became the first American woman to win three gold medals in track at the same Olympics. The little girl who had been told she would never walk was now the fastest woman runner in the world!

Wilma retired from running in 1962. She became a second-grade teacher and a high school track coach. She started the Wilma Rudolph Foundation, which teaches young athletes that they, too, can be champions.

1962
Wilma retires from running.

1981
She starts the Wilma Rudolph Foundation.

1983
Wilma is elected to the U.S. Olympic Hall of Fame.

1994
She dies on November 12, in Brentwood, Tennessee.

Narrating

Write a Biography

Choose a person you want to know more about. That person might be an explorer, a president, or a sports star. Look up facts about the person in books, in the encyclopedia, or on the Internet. Write a biography of the person.

Tips

- **Write an interesting beginning for the biography.**
- **Tell about the person's early life first. Then tell about the person's later years.**
- **Write a title that will get a reader's attention.**

Former President Jimmy Carter helps build houses for people.

Yo-Yo Ma plays the cello.

Get to Know These People

Helen Keller: Courage in the Dark
by Johanna Hurwitz (Random)
Helen Keller overcame the challenges of blindness and deafness with the help of a teacher.

Happy Birthday, Martin Luther King
by Jean Marzollo (Scholastic)
This great leader made the United States a better place for all people.

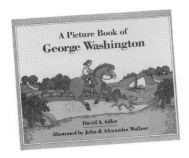

A Picture Book of George Washington
by David A. Adler (Holiday)
The first president of the United States is known as the "Father of Our Country."

Roberto Clemente: Athlete and Hero
by Diana Pérez, Ph.D. (Modern Curriculum)
A boy grows up to become a famous baseball player, but always helps people in need.

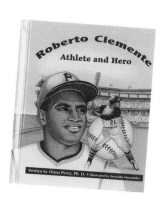

Talent Show

My music
reaches
to the sky.

Chippewa proverb

Talent Show

Contents

Phonics Library

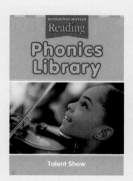

- **Our Classroom Zoo Book**
- **Jade's Drumming**
- **Dwight the Knight**
- **Who Drew the Cartoon?**
- **Will Holly Sing?**
- **Fright Night**

Big Book

Cleveland Lee's Beale Street Band
by Art Flowers

Theme Paperbacks

Annie's Gifts
by Angela Shelf Medearis

Spotlight on Cody
by Betsy Duffey

On My Way Practice Reader

The Garden
by Lee S. Justice

Book Links

If you like . . .

The Art Lesson
by Tomie dePaola

Then try . . .

The Legend of the Indian Paintbrush
by Tomie dePaola (Putnam)

Little Gopher looks for a way to paint the colors of the sunset.

What Do Illustrators Do?
by Eileen Christelow (Clarion)

Two artists create different versions of the story "Jack and the Beanstalk."

If you like . . .

Moses Goes to a Concert
by Isaac Millman

Then try . . .

Mole Music
by David McPhail (Holt)

After much practice, Mole learns to play beautiful music on his violin.

Music, Music for Everyone
by Vera B. Williams (Greenwillow)

To raise money, Rosa and her friends form the Oak Street Band.

If you like . . .

The School Mural
by Sarah Vázquez

Then try . . .

The Chalk Box Kid

by Clyde Robert Bulla (Random)

When his family moves to a new house, Gregory amuses himself by drawing a garden.

The Riddle Streak

by Susan Beth Pfeffer (Holt)

Amy searches for a way to do something better than her brother.

Technology

At Education Place

Post your reviews of these books or see what others had to say.

Education Place®
www.eduplace.com/kids

• • •

At school

Read at school and take a quiz.

Accelerated Reader®

• • •

At home

Read at home and log on to

www.bookadventure.org

Be an Artist

The Art Lesson is the story of a boy who wants to be an artist when he grows up. What would you need to be an artist? It depends on what kind of art you want to make.

Crayons are great for making brightly colored drawings.

Many artists like to draw with chalk.

Some paints are made by adding water to colored powders.

Art students sometimes **copy** famous paintings or illustrations. It takes a lot of **practice** to become a good artist.

When you paint, it's a good idea to wear a **smock** to protect your clothes!

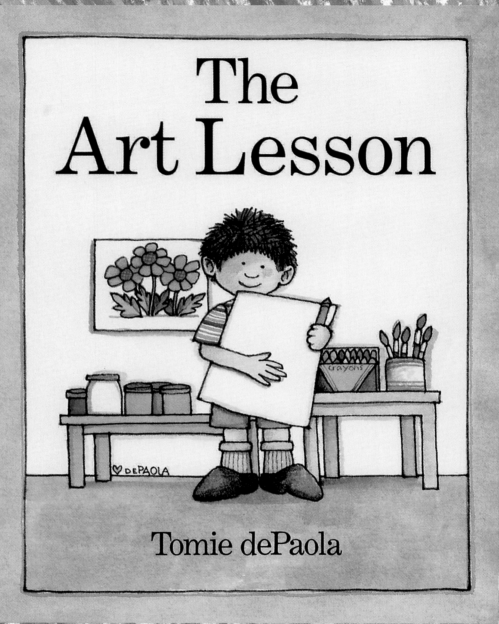

The Art Lesson

Tomie dePaola

Strategy Focus

As you read about a boy who loves to draw pictures, **evaluate** the way the author uses words and pictures to tell the story.

Tommy knew he wanted to be an artist
when he grew up. He drew pictures
everywhere he went. It was his favorite thing
to do.

His friends had favorite things to do, too.
Jack collected all kinds of turtles. Herbie
made huge cities in his sandbox. Jeannie,
Tommy's best friend, could do cartwheels
and stand on her head.

But Tommy drew and drew and drew.

His twin cousins, who were already
grown up, were in art school learning to be
real artists. They told him not to copy and
to practice, practice, practice. So, he did.

Tommy put his pictures up on the walls
of his half of the bedroom.
His mom put them up all around the house.

His dad took them to the barber shop
where he worked.

Tom and Nana, Tommy's Irish grandfather
and grandmother, had his pictures in their
grocery store.

Nana-Fall-River, his Italian grandmother,
put one in a special frame on the table next
to the photograph of Aunt Clo in her
wedding dress.

Once Tommy took a flashlight and a pencil under the covers and drew pictures on his sheets. But when his mom changed the sheets on Monday and found them, she said, "No more drawing on the sheets, Tommy."

His mom and dad were having a new house built, so Tommy drew pictures of what it would look like when it was finished.

When the walls were up, one of the carpenters gave Tommy a piece of bright blue chalk. Tommy took the chalk and drew beautiful pictures all over the unfinished walls.

But, when the painters came, his dad said, "That's it, Tommy. No more drawing on the walls."

Tommy couldn't wait to go to kindergarten.
His brother, Joe, told him there was a real art
teacher who came to the school to give
ART LESSONS!

"When do we have our art lessons?"
Tommy asked the kindergarten teacher.

"Oh, you won't have your art lessons until
next year," said Miss Bird. "But, we are going
to paint pictures tomorrow."

It wasn't much fun.

The paint was awful and the paper got all
wrinkly. Miss Bird made the paint by pouring
different colored powders into different jars
and mixing them with water. The paint didn't
stick to the paper very well and it cracked.

If it was windy when Tommy carried
his picture home, the paint blew right off
the paper.

"At least you get more than one piece of
paper in kindergarten," his brother, Joe, said.
"When the art teacher comes, you only get
one piece."

Tommy knew that the art teacher came to
the school every other Wednesday. He could
tell she was an artist because she wore a blue
smock over her dress and she always carried a
big box of thick colored chalks.

Once, Tommy and Jeannie looked at the
drawings that were hung up in the hallway.
They were done by the first graders.

"Your pictures are much better," Jeannie
told Tommy. "Next year when we have real art
lessons, you'll be the best one!"

Tommy could hardly wait. He practiced all summer. Then, on his birthday, which was right after school began, his mom and dad gave him a box of sixty-four Crayola crayons. Regular boxes of crayons had red, orange, yellow, green, blue, violet, brown and black. This box had so many other colors: blue-violet, turquoise, red-orange, pink and even gold, silver and copper.

"Class," said Miss Landers, the first-grade teacher, "next month, the art teacher will come to our room, so on Monday instead of Singing, we will practice using our crayons."

On Monday, Tommy brought his sixty-four crayons to school. Miss Landers was not pleased. "Everyone must use the same crayons," she said.

"SCHOOL CRAYONS!"

School crayons had only the same old eight colors. As Miss Landers passed them out to the class, she said, "These crayons are school property, so do not break them, peel off the paper, or wear down the points."

"How am I supposed to practice being an artist with SCHOOL CRAYONS?" Tommy asked Jack and Herbie.

"That's enough, Tommy," Miss Landers said. "And I want you to take those birthday crayons home with you and leave them there."

And Joe was right. They only got ONE piece of paper.

Finally, the day of the art lesson came. Tommy could hardly sleep that night.

The next morning, he hid the box of sixty-four crayons under his sweater and went off to school. He was ready!

The classroom door opened and in walked
the art teacher. Miss Landers said, "Class, this
is Mrs. Bowers, the art teacher. Patty, who is
our paper monitor this week, will give out one
piece of paper to each of you. And remember,
don't ruin it because it is the only piece you'll
get. Now, pay attention to Mrs. Bowers."

"Class," Mrs. Bowers began, "because Thanksgiving is not too far away, we will learn to draw a Pilgrim man, a Pilgrim woman and a turkey. Watch carefully and copy me."

Copy? COPY? Tommy knew that real
artists didn't copy.

This was terrible. This was supposed to be
a real art lesson. He folded his arms and just
sat there. "Now what's the matter?" Miss
Landers asked. Tommy looked past her and
spoke right to Mrs. Bowers.

"I'm going to be an artist when I grow up
and my cousins told me that real artists don't
copy. And besides, Miss Landers won't let me
use my own sixty-four Crayola crayons."

"Well, well," Mrs. Bowers said. "What are we going to do?" She turned to Miss Landers and they whispered together. Miss Landers nodded.

"Now, Tommy," Mrs. Bowers said. "It wouldn't be fair to let you do something different from the rest of the class.

"But, I have an idea. If you draw the Pilgrim man and woman and the turkey, and if there's any time left, I'll give you another piece of paper and you can do your own picture with your own crayons. Can you do that?"

"I'll try," Tommy said, with a big smile.

And he did.

And he did.

And he still does.

Meet the Author and Illustrator

Tomie dePaola

Other Books

The Baby Sister

The Legend of the Indian Paintbrush

26 Fairmont Avenue

Fact File

- Tomie dePaola's name is pronounced like this: Tommy da-POW-la
- He grew up in Meriden, Connecticut, and many of his stories are about his childhood there. He based the story of *The Art Lesson* on his own life.
- When he was a child, some of his favorite things to do were drawing, painting, writing poetry, and tap-dancing.
- He uses tempera, watercolor, and acrylic paints for his illustrations.

Tomie dePaola wrote *The Art Lesson* for his favorite art teacher, the real Mrs. Beulah Bowers. To find out about the true story behind *The Art Lesson,* visit Education Place.

www.eduplace.com/kids

Responding

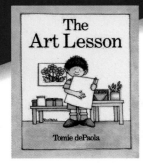

The
Art Lesson
Tomie dePaola

Think About the Selection

1. Why do you think Tomie dePaola wrote this story?

2. Tommy's cousins told him not to copy. What do you think of their advice?

3. Why do you think Tommy decided to take his birthday crayons back to school?

4. What do you think Miss Landers and Mrs. Bowers were whispering about?

5. **Connecting/Comparing** How did some of the other characters in the story feel about Tommy's talent for drawing?

Informing

Write an Invitation

Write an invitation to an art show at your school. Tell a friend all about your art show.

Tips

- Tell where and when the show will take place.
- Use adjectives to make the show sound interesting.

Art

Draw a Job

Make a list of five things that you like to do. Then choose one that you could do as a job when you grow up. Draw a picture of yourself doing that job.

Listening and Speaking

Role-Play a Conversation

With a partner, role-play a conversation between Tommy and one of his teachers. Use your voice to show how each character is feeling.

Internet

Take an Online Poll

Is art your favorite subject in school? Do you want to be an artist when you grow up? What is your favorite book by Tomie dePaola? Take our online poll to tell us.

www.eduplace.com/kids

321

Skill: How to Look at Fine Art

When you look at a painting or a picture, ask yourself questions such as:

❶ What is the **subject** of the painting?

❷ What **colors** does the artist use?

❸ Does the picture tell a **story**?

❹ What **materials** did the artist use?

Carmen Lomas Garza

Look carefully at the painting on the right. You see a family working together in a kitchen. You may have noticed the bright colors and patterns. Did you also see the keys hanging on the wall?

Look again. You probably noticed something else that you didn't see the first time you looked. The picture you are looking at was painted by Carmen Lomas Garza. Carmen's paintings are so full of interesting details that you can look at them over and over again, and always find something new.

Tamalada (Making Tamales), 1987

Carmen taught herself to draw by practicing every day. She would draw whatever was in front of her — books, cats, her left hand, her sisters and brothers, paper bags, flowers. Carmen drew anything or anybody that would stay still for a few minutes.

Guacamole, 1989

One painting may be a picture of people dancing at a party. Another may show Carmen and members of her family picking fruit, celebrating a birthday, or just getting together to cook food. Sometimes, she even includes the family cat, or a lizard she might have seen crawling on the porch.

Naranjas (Oranges), 1990

Carmen's work has been shown in museums all around the country. She has also written popular books for children. Carmen hopes that her paintings and books will help people learn more about her Mexican-American culture.

Instructions

The purpose of writing instructions is to tell others how to do or make something. Use this student's writing as a model when you write instructions of your own.

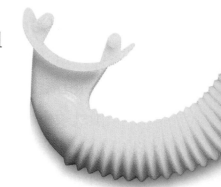

The **title** tells what the instructions are about.

Sometimes it is good to **introduce** your instructions topic.

How to Snorkel

If you like to swim and see an interesting underwater world, then you might want to try snorkeling. It is fun to snorkel anywhere. You can snorkel in your bathtub, a swimming pool, or a lake. Snorkeling is a nature sport where you wear a clear mask and a special underwater breathing device called a snorkel.

To snorkel, you need a snorkel, mask, and fins. The first step is to slide the mask securely over your forehead and nose. Next, put the mouthpiece in your mouth. Make sure the snorkel tube is above your head so when you swim the snorkel is above the surface of the water. Then put your fins on your feet.

Finally, start swimming on your belly, and breathe through the snorkel tube. Now it is time for the fun part. Look for the amazing underwater world. You may see plants, rocks, fish, someone's feet, or even your bathtub drain!

> Good instructions tell what to do in a clear **order**.

> Use **time-order words** to show the reader what to do first, next, and last.

Meet the Author

Bryan O.

Grade: two

State: California

Hobbies: reading nonfiction books, collecting sports cards, and swimming

What he'd like to be when he grows up: a scientist or a pastor

Communicating with Sign Language

A person who is **deaf** is someone who is either partly or completely unable to hear. In the story you are about to read, a deaf boy and his classmates go to a concert.

How does a person without the sense of **hearing** enjoy music or talk to someone? Deaf people are able to make music a part of their lives because they can feel the **vibrations** that certain **instruments**, such as drums or tubas, make.

To communicate with other people, a person who is deaf may **sign** the things he or she wants to say. Signing is a type of language made up of hand movements.

In the story *Moses Goes to a Concert*, the character named Marjorie Elwyn is based on this real-life musician, Evelyn Glennie.

Manual Alphabet

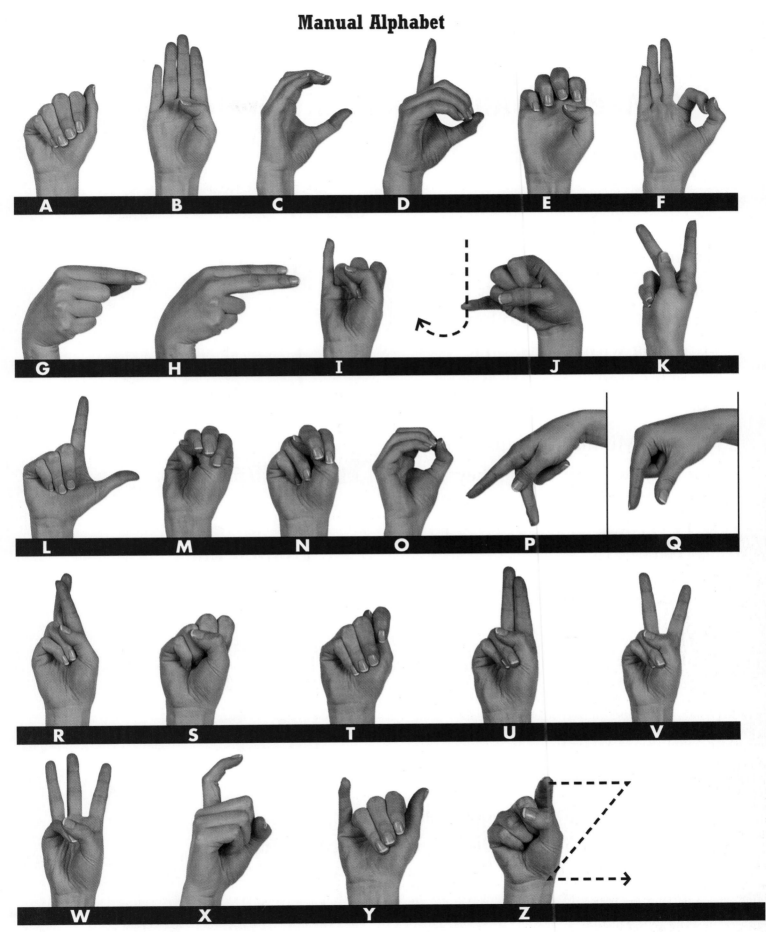

329

Meet the Author and Illustrator

Isaac Millman

Isaac Millman started writing because it made the stories he drew seem more alive. He says that writing, to him, is "drawing with words." He takes his stories from things he sees around him.

Mr. Millman and his wife live in New York City. They have been married forty years and have two grown sons and a grandson. *Moses Goes to a Concert* is Mr. Millman's first book, but he plans to write many more.

Another Book Illustrated by Isaac Millman:
Howie Bowles, Secret Agent

To find out more about Isaac Millman, visit Education Place. **www.eduplace.com/kids**

330

A boy who is deaf goes to a concert with his classmates. As you read, stop to **summarize** the important facts in the story.

Moses plays on his new drum.

He can't hear the sounds he is making because he is deaf, but he feels the vibration of the drum through his hands. He has taken off his shoes so he can feel it through his feet, too.

| I | PLAY | THE DRUM |

Today, Moses is going on a field trip. His teacher, Mr. Samuels, is taking him and his classmates, who are all deaf, to a young people's concert.

As the children climb onto the bus, they wonder what is inside Mr. Samuels's black bag.

"A big surprise," signs Mr. Samuels.

THE TEACHER

HAS

A BIG SURPRISE

On the bus, Moses signs to his friend. "John!
My parents gave me a new drum!"
John signs back. "I got one, too!"

MY

FRIEND

1

2

Children from all over the city are coming to the concert. Moses and his friend John wait for their class to get off the bus so they can go inside together.

Mr. Samuels leads them to their seats in the first row. Across the stage, in front of the orchestra, are all the percussion instruments.

"Children, the percussionist is a friend of mine," signs Mr. Samuels.

A LOUD MUSICAL SOUND

"What's a percussionist?" Anna signs back.

"A musician who plays an instrument such as a drum, cymbals, even a piano," replies Mr. Samuels.

A young woman walks onto the stage. Everyone stands up to applaud. Some of Moses's classmates wave instead of clapping. The percussionist smiles and bows to the audience.

WE	WAVE	AND	APPLAUD

"She has no shoes!" Moses signs in surprise.

The teacher smiles and signs, "She is deaf, too. She follows the orchestra by feeling the vibrations of the music through her stocking feet."

Then Mr. Samuels takes eleven balloons out of his black bag and hands one to each of his students.

"Oh! What beautiful balloons!"
Anna signs.

"Hold them on your laps," signs Mr.
Samuels. "They'll help you feel the music."

ELEVEN	BEAUTIFUL	BALLOONS

The conductor turns to face the orchestra and
raises his baton. The percussionist strikes the huge
gong and the concert begins.

The percussionist watches the conductor and moves from one instrument to the next, striking each to make a sound. Moses and his classmates hold their balloons in their laps. They can feel the music as their balloons pick up the vibrations.

I FEEL VIBRATIONS

When the concert is over, Mr. Samuels has another surprise. He takes the children onstage to meet his friend, Ms. Marjorie Elwyn. "She will tell you how she became a percussionist," signs Mr. Samuels.

| [MY] FRIENDS | AND | I | ARE DEAF |

351

"I became seriously ill at the age of seven," signs Ms. Elwyn. "And when I recovered, I found out that I had lost my hearing. I was deaf."

"What did you do then?" signs Moses.

I   WORKED HARD.

MY

HEART

WAS SET ON

BECOMING

A PERCUSSIONIST

AND

I

DID.

"Now you can play on my musical instruments,"
Ms. Elwyn signs. "Come with me, children."

Ann plays on the marimba . . .
Beverly strikes the triangle . . .

Mark pounds the floor tom and the cymbal . . .
Dianne beats the tom-toms . . . John hits the snare
drum . . . and Moses thumps the bass drum . . .

David strikes the gong . . . Tommy and Suzy play
on the tubular bells . . . while Steve bangs the
kettledrum and Maria plays the congas.

"Children! We have to go!" Mr. Samuels announces after a while. "Ms. Elwyn has to get ready for another concert."

Moses and his classmates sign thank you, and they wave goodbye to Ms. Elwyn.

THANKS GOODBYE

On the bus on the way home, Moses signs, "It was so much fun!"

SO MUCH   FUN

That night, Moses tells his parents about the concert. Here is what he says:

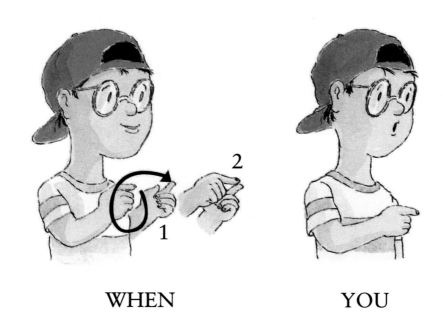

WHEN   YOU

SET YOUR MIND TO IT,

YOU CAN BECOME

ANYTHING YOU WANT

WHEN YOU GROW UP . . .

A DOCTOR,

ARTIST,

TEACHER,

LAWYER,

FARMER,

ELECTRICIAN,

OR

ACTOR.

I

WANT

TO BECOME

A PERCUSSIONIST.

Responding

Think About the Selection

1. Why do you think Ms. Elwyn shares her experiences with Moses' class?

2. Which details helped you understand how Moses and his classmates were able to enjoy the concert?

3. What does Moses mean when he says, "When you set your mind to it, you can become anything you want . . ."?

4. Think of a concert you have gone to or music you have heard. How is your experience the same as Moses'? How is it different?

5. **Connecting/Comparing** Compare Mr. Samuels to the teachers in *The Art Lesson*.

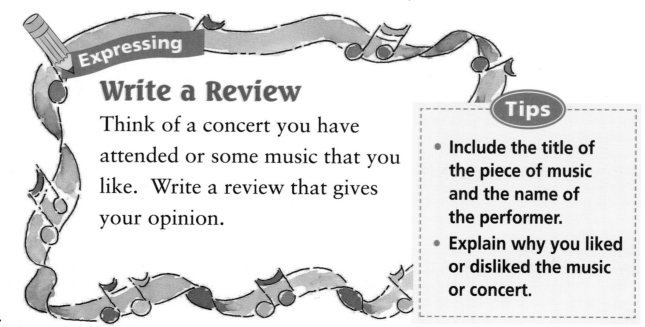

Expressing

Write a Review

Think of a concert you have attended or some music that you like. Write a review that gives your opinion.

> **Tips**
> - Include the title of the piece of music and the name of the performer.
> - Explain why you liked or disliked the music or concert.

Science

Experiment with Sounds

Stretch a rubber band over a cup's opening. Gently pluck the rubber band, then squeeze the cup gently to change its shape. Pluck the rubber band again. When you change the cup's shape, how does the sound change?

Social Studies

Sign Your Name

Study the hand alphabet on page 329. Practice spelling your name. Then sign the letters of your name to a partner.

Bonus **Sign your partner's name.**

Internet

E-mail a Friend

What did you like about *Moses Goes to a Concert*? Is there anything you didn't like? Send an e-mail to a friend. Tell him or her about the story.

www.eduplace.com/kids

Social Studies Link

Skill: How to Read a Concert Program

When you read a concert program, look for the following information:

- The title of the concert, and the date and time are usually listed first.

- The **performers** are the singers or musicians onstage.

- The **composer** wrote the music or words.

Go to a Concert

by Avery Hart and Paul Mantell

If you've never been to a concert, are you ever in for a treat! A concert is a chance to hear musicians playing the music they know best.

You can find out about what concerts are coming up in the area by checking the entertainment section of the newspaper. Free concerts are usually advertised on library bulletin boards. There are usually a lot of free concerts in the summer when they can be held in parks, and also at holiday time, when schools and community orchestras like to perform. Ask a grown-up to take you to one.

North Elementary School Spring Recital

May 21, 7:30 p.m.
Directed by: Mr. Dawe

Green Speckled Frogs

by Raffi   Performed by Ms. Cronin's first grade class

Swallowed a Fly

by Alan Mills   Performed by Mr. Lim's second grade class

Erie Canal

by Thomas S. Allen   Performed by Mrs. Serpa's third grade class

Be sure to arrive early enough to get a good seat, in case there is open seating, which is first come, first served. During the performance, sit back, turn on your imagination, and enjoy. The only rule is "No Talking, Please" — at a concert, it's the musicians who get to make the noise!

At folk and rock concerts, you can show your appreciation by clapping along with the music. At a classical concert, save your reaction for the end — even if the musicians take occasional pauses during their performances. But at the end of a classical concert, clap as hard as you wish. You can even stand up and shout "Bravo!" if you think the music was absolutely wonderful.

A Mural

A **mural** is a large painting done on a wall or sometimes on a ceiling. Making a mural can be a big **event**. **Sketches**, or plans for the painting, have to be made before painting can begin.

In some cases, a team of people will work together to create a mural. Working on a big **project** like a mural can be more than fun. It can also be a way for people to show their **pride**, especially if the mural shows a **scene** that is important to the community where it is painted.

In the story you are about to read, a group of schoolchildren make a mural that shows just how they feel about their school.

371

The School Mural

Written by
Sarah Vázquez

Illustrated by
Melinda Levine

Strategy Focus

A group of schoolchildren work together to show their school pride. As you read the story, think of **questions** to ask about their experience.

1
The News

One morning, Mrs. Sanchez greeted her class. "I have some news. Soon our school will be fifty years old. We're going to have an open house on May twenty-fifth to celebrate this big event."

Mrs. Sanchez said, "Each class will make a big project. It should be about our school and our community."

Paul asked, "What should we do?"

"I'm sure you'll think of some good ideas," said Mrs. Sanchez.

The class went outside for recess. Mei Lee
(MAY-lee) and Paul raced for the swings. They liked
to see who could swing the highest.

Mei Lee thought about the big project. She said,
"I think we should write a song or put on a play for
our class project. What do you think?"

Paul said, "We've done those things before. We need a really big project."

While Mei Lee was swinging very high, she looked past the school. She saw the building across the street. It had a big mural painted on the front wall. This gave her a great idea.

2
A Mural Idea

Later that day, Mrs. Sanchez asked the class for their ideas. Paul wanted to print a huge banner on the computer. Maria wanted to make bookmarks to give away. Edwina's idea was to make a huge card and have everyone sign it. Mei Lee said, "Let's make a mural."

"What's a mural?" asked Ted.

"It's a big picture painted on the wall of a building," said Mei Lee. "Look at this one at the pet shop." She pointed out the window.

Mrs. Sanchez listed the children's ideas on the board. "These are all good ideas," said Mrs. Sanchez. "Let's pick one that everyone can have a part in. Look over the list again. Then we'll vote on our project."

Mrs. Sanchez pointed to each idea as they voted. At first, not many children voted. Then, she pointed to the mural idea. Sixteen children raised their hands!

"I think you picked a fine project that everyone can work on," said Mrs. Sanchez.

banner
bookmarks
card
mural
song
play

3
The Plan

Mrs. Sanchez said, "People from many different cultures have painted on walls. Long ago, cave people painted on the walls of their caves. Their paintings tell us how people lived then. Here is a picture of a cave painting. It is a kind of mural." She held up the picture.

"Murals are huge! We'll need to think of lots of things to show," said Maria.

Mrs. Sanchez said, "Murals tell about people and their community. Think of some things to tell about your school."

"Let's tell people about our school band," said Beto.

"We'll need a really big wall for our mural," said Maria.

"What about the outside wall we see when we swing on the playground?" said Paul. "All the classes see it every day!"

Mrs. Sanchez said, "I'll ask our principal, Mr. Ford, if it's OK. Mei Lee, since the mural was your idea, please go with me to see him."

Later, Mrs. Sanchez said, "The principal likes the idea of painting a mural on the wall. He said he will ask if the local newspaper will take a picture of the mural. That would show how our community works together."

Beto asked, "Where will we get the paint? We'll need lots of brushes, too."

Paul said, "Let's ask the art teacher for help. Maybe we could ask our families to help us, too. My mom loves to paint."

"Good idea. Please tell your families about our project, and then I'll call them," said Mrs. Sanchez.

For the next three weeks, the class worked on the
mural. First, they planned the scenes to draw. Next,
the art teacher helped the children draw sketches of
the different scenes on the wall.

Then they started painting the mural. Twenty
children couldn't all paint at once, so they took
turns. First the band group painted. Then the next
group painted. Some parents helped paint the high
parts of the wall near the roof. It was hard work, but
everyone had fun.

Some funny things happened. One day, Paul bumped the paint tray and got paint all over himself. Then he slipped and put his hands on the wall. He left his handprints on the mural! Everyone decided it looked good, so they added their handprints, too.

Another time, Anjelina was painting high up on a ladder. She dipped the brush into the bucket and splattered lots of paint onto the wall. But down below her was Beto, so she splattered him, too! He had green hair that day.

5
The Newspaper

When the mural was finished, Mr. Ford called the newspaper. A reporter came to write a story. He asked the class many questions about how they made the mural. He got everyone's name. He took photos of the mural with the painters in front of it. He told the children to watch for the article soon.

The children could hardly wait to see the article in the newspaper. After about a week, the article appeared with a big photo of the mural. The headline said, "Children Show School Pride."

6
The Open House

On the day of the open house, Mr. Ford spoke to all the children, parents, and visitors. He told everyone what project each class had done. Then he invited the visitors to walk around and see all the projects. The children were very proud and excited.

When Mr. Ford told about the mural, the crowd cheered. One neighbor stood up and thanked the students for making such a beautiful painting. He said people would enjoy it for many years.

The newspaper reporter came again, too. He took pictures of the mural and the children.

Some of the children decided they liked
painting so much that it became their new hobby.
Someday they might be famous painters. Or maybe
they'll come back to the school sometime just to
enjoy their mural. They might even tell students
the story of how their mural came to be.

Meet the Author and the Illustrator

Meet the Author
Sarah Vázquez

One afternoon while in a public park, Sarah Vázquez and her son, Manuel, saw a wall covered with graffiti. They thought that the children who played in the park should have something better to look at. Ms. Vázquez wrote *The School Mural* to tell a story about what can happen when people decide to make things better for their community.

Meet the Illustrator
Melinda Levine

Melinda Levine lives in Oakland, California, with her husband, teenage daughter, gray silky cat, and big fluffy dog. She created the many-layered collages for *The School Mural* using cut paper, glue, scissors, and other paper-cutting tools.

Other books illustrated by Melinda Levine:
The Stone Soup Book of Friendship Stories
Water for One, Water for Everyone

Learn more about Sarah Vázquez and Melinda Levine, and about the ancient craft of paper cutting. Visit Education Place. **www.eduplace.com/kids**

Think About the Selection

1. Why do you think most of the children voted for Mei Lee's idea?

2. Why is a mural a good way to show school or community pride?

3. How do you think the adults felt about helping with the school mural?

4. If you could plan and paint a mural for your school, what would it show? Why?

5. Connecting/Comparing How might Tommy from *The Art Lesson* have helped make the mural?

Informing

Write Newspaper Headlines

A reporter wrote an article about the school mural. The headline said "Children Show School Pride." Think of other headlines the reporter could have used. Write headlines for his article.

Tips

- Look at real newspaper headlines for ideas.
- Don't include words such as *the* and *a* in your headlines.

Math

Make Estimates

Find walls in your classroom or school which might be good places for a mural. Estimate the height and length of the walls. Record your estimates. Then use a yardstick to measure. Record the measurements.

Bonus List your measurements from longest to shortest.

Walls	Height	Length
classroom	10 ft.	12 ft.
hallway		

Viewing

Give a Presentation

Look carefully at the mural in the story. Present it to a classmate or small group. Describe what is in the mural and explain why the students chose to include those scenes.

Internet

Take a Web Tour

Learn more about different types of art and the artists who make it. Visit Education Place and take a Web tour of an art museum.

www.eduplace.com/kids

Skill: How to Read a Comic Strip

- Comic strips usually show dialogue inside **speech balloons**.

- Most comic strips show **scenes** in boxes.

- If a comic strip has more than one row of boxes, read each row from left to right, and then from top to bottom.

PEANUTS
BY CHARLES M. SCHULZ

OUR TEACHER SAYS WE HAVE TO MEASURE SOMETHING WITH A RULER

HOLD STILL...I'LL TRY MEASURING YOUR MOUTH AGAIN...

HMM...ONE LIP IS ON THE SIX AND THE OTHER LIP IS ON THE NINE...

I WONDER HOW YOU WRITE THAT... I'LL PUT, "LIP TO LIP, THREE INCHES"

I CAN'T STAND IT!

Calvin and Hobbes
BY BILL WATTERSON

WOW! NOBODY IS ON THE SWINGS! I CAN'T BELIEVE IT!

HA HA! I ALMOST *NEVER* GET A SWING AT RECESS!

THIS IS GREAT!

NO ONE IS TELLING ME TO HURRY UP!

HIGHER! HIGHER!

WHEE!

..EITHER THIS IS MY LUCKY DAY, OR I MISSED THE END-OF-RECESS BELL AGAIN.

✔ Writing a Personal Narrative

A test may ask you to write about something that really happened to you. Read this sample test item. Then use the tips when you write a personal narrative.

> **Write about a time when you used a talent that you have.**

Here is a planning chart that one student made.

I will write about a summer swim meet.	
What happened: I swam in a meet.	
Race 1: I won the race.	Detail: Three boys swam too.
Race 2: I came in last.	Detail: I had trouble at the end.
Race 3: I got second place.	Detail: Beth came in first.

Tips

- Read the test item carefully. Look for key words that tell you what to write about.
- Plan your narrative before you write. Make a chart to help you plan.
- After you finish writing, proofread your narrative.

Here is a good personal narrative that the same student wrote.

My Best Swim Meet

Last Saturday I swam in the best swim meet I've had. I practiced for a week. Mom and Dad went with me. I swam three times in the meet.

My first race was hard. Three boys swam too. I was so excited! I won first place. I came in last in the second race because I was tired at the end. But it did not matter because I tried my best.

Beth, two boys I don't know, and Varum swam in the last race. My friend Beth won. I got second place. I think I'm a good swimmer because I practice a lot. I can't wait to swim in the next meet.

The beginning makes the reader want to keep reading.

Details tell what, who, why, when, and where.

The last part tells how the writer felt, or what the writer learned.

There are few grammar, spelling, capitalization, or punctuation mistakes.

Glossary

This glossary can help you find the meanings of some of the words in this book. The meanings given are the meanings of the words as they are used in the book. Sometimes a second meaning is also given.

A

accept
To say yes to: *I accept your offer of a new puppy.*

accident
Something you did not want or expect to happen: *Harry had an accident on his bicycle and fell down.*

advantage
Anything that is a help in getting what someone or something wants: *Frogs have the advantage of long, sticky tongues to catch fast flying insects.*

angry
Unhappy with someone; mad: *Tyler got angry when his sister dropped his glass.*

antennae
A pair of thin organs on the head of insects that can be used to touch and smell: *An ant's antennae can help it find food.*

antennae

argument
A talk between people who do not agree and are mad at each other: *Miko had an argument with Leah over whose painting was better.*

attention

The act of looking and listening with care: *We paid close attention to the teacher as she read the story.*

audience

The people who gather to hear or see something: *A large audience sat in the theater waiting to see the movie.*

B

bakery

A place where foods such as bread and cake are made or sold: *The new bakery makes the best doughnuts.*

bakery

bolt

A flash of lightning: *The bolt of lightning was so bright it lit up my bedroom.*

C

chalk

A writing tool made mostly from seashells and used to write on blackboards or other surfaces: *Keisha used green chalk to draw pictures on the board.*

chalk

cocoon

Silky covering made by some insects to protect themselves until fully grown: *The caterpillars curled up in their* **cocoons** *and waited to grow.*

cocoon

colony

A group of animals, plants, or people living or growing together: *Ants live together in large* **colonies**.

command

An order: *I taught our dog the* **commands***, "sit" and "speak."*

copy

To make another of something: *Everyone had to* **copy** *the letters of the alphabet from the board.*

crayon

A stick of colored wax used for drawing or writing: *Each box had eight* **crayons** *in it.*

crayons

culture

The things that a group of people do and think and the laws that the group lives by: *Sports like baseball are a part of our* **culture**.

customer

Person who often buys goods or services: *Ms. Ames is one of the* **customers** *who come into the coffee shop every morning.*

D

deaf

Unable to hear: *Mrs. Li watches your lips when you speak to her because she is* **deaf**.

distract

To make someone less interested in one thing and more interested in another: *My mother has to* **distract** *me from looking at the needle when I get my flu shot.*

dough

A thick mixture of flour and liquid that is used to make bread and other baked foods: *We cut the cookie* **dough** *into animal shapes.*

dough

E

event

Something that happens: *The first* **event** *of the party was a game of tag.*

F

fungus

A group of living things that are not plants or animals and have no flowers, leaves, or green coloring: *A mushroom is a type of fungus.*

fungus

fuss

To complain needlessly: *My aunt used to fuss about getting dirt on the porch.*

fussed

Form of **fuss**: *Jorge fussed about not getting any ice cream.*

G

groan

To make a deep sound low in the throat to show pain or anger: *I groan when I have an earache.*

groaned

Form of **groan**: *Kai groaned when the dentist told her she had a cavity.*

grumble

To say things in an unhappy tone: *We heard our dad grumble when he found the broken lamp.*

grumbled

Form of **grumble**: *Jenny grumbled when she was sent to bed early.*

grumpily

Acting in a cranky or upset way: *Andre grumpily got out of the pool when his mother called him to go to bed.*

guard

Watch over and keep safe: *My sister likes to eat my cookies, so I **guard** them when she's around.*

guarded

Form of **guard**: *The dog **guarded** the front door so no one could get past it.*

H

hearing

The sense by which sound is picked up; ability to hear: *My dog's sense of **hearing** is very good.*

horizon

The line along which the earth and the sky appear to meet: *Before night fell, the sun sat like a big orange ball on the **horizon**.*

I

ingredient

Part that makes up a mixture: *We bought all the **ingredients** we needed to make pumpkin pie.*

instrument

Thing that is used in making music: *Flutes are **instruments** that make high and soft sounds.*

L

larvae

Newly hatched insects that have no wings and look like worms: *Caterpillars are **larvae** that grow into butterflies and moths.*

larva

lightning

The flash of light in the sky in the middle of a storm: *The bright **lightning** lit up the sky.*

lightning

M

mural

A painting that is done on a wall or a ceiling: *The **mural** on the classroom wall was drawn by the students.*

N

newborn

Just brought into life: *My **newborn** baby brother hasn't left the hospital yet.*

O

officer

A member of a police force: *The **officer** made sure everyone at the parade was safe.*

officer

P

penalty

A punishment for breaking a rule or losing a game or sport: *The **penalty** for breaking the fire drill rules is no after-school sports.*

percussion

Musical instruments that create a special sound when struck: *Drums are **percussion** instruments.*

percussion

pest

A person or thing that is not nice to be around: *That fly is a **pest** because it keeps buzzing around my head.*

powder

Very small pieces of something: *That clown's face is covered with many different colored **powders**.*

practice

To do something over and over in order to be good at it: *Lelia and Rashawn **practice** jumping rope every day.*

pride

A feeling of happiness about something you or someone close to you has done: *Gino's parents were full of **pride** because he had learned to read so quickly.*

project

A special study or experiment done by students: *The class made a model of a volcano for their science **project**.*

promise

Say that you will do something: *I **promise** that I will always pick up my room.*

promised

Form of **promise**: *We promised to wash the car next Saturday.*

Q

quarrel

A talk between people who cannot agree and are mad at each other: *Marta and Joe had a quarrel about cleaning up after dinner.*

R

recipe

A set of directions for making something, usually food: *Gia wrote the recipe for oatmeal cookies on the board.*

recipe

ruin

To harm something so that it cannot be fixed: *Grape juice can ruin a white shirt.*

rumble

Make a deep rolling sound: *We listen to the train rumble by our house every night.*

rumbled

Form of **rumble**: *The big truck rumbled down the highway.*

S

safety

Freedom from danger or harm: *We follow school safety rules so that no one gets hurt.*

scene

Place, picture, or drawing of a place or thing as seen by a viewer: *The postcards from Grandpa have scenes from Italy on them.*

sign

Use hand motions to express thoughts: *I will **sign** the news to the children, since they can't hear it for themselves.*

signs

Form of **sign**: *Sam **signs** with his hands to tell stories to children who can't hear.*

sketch

A picture drawn with lines but not colored in: *My parents made many **sketches** of our house before it was built.*

smock

A long shirt or apron worn over clothes to keep them clean: *We used an old shirt as a **smock** when we painted.*

spread

To cover something with something else: *Shaily **spread** butter on her toast.*

T

teenage

Between the ages of thirteen and nineteen: *Since Mary started going to her new school, she has lots of **teenage** friends.*

thunder

The deep, loud noise that comes from the sky during a storm: *The **thunder** was so loud we couldn't hear each other.*

tunnel

Underground or underwater passageway: *Some animals dig **tunnels** underground.*

tunnel

twin

Two children born at one birth: *My cousins are **twins**, and they look exactly like each other.*

twins

V

vibration

Rapid movement back and forth or up and down: *The **vibration** of the table was caused by the earthquake.*

W

weather

The state of the atmosphere at a given time or place, including heat, cold, rain, and wind: *Since the **weather** was warm and sunny, we had a picnic in the park.*

Acknowledgments

Main Literature Selections

Ant, by Rebecca Stefoff. Text copyright © 1998 by Rebecca Stefoff. Reprinted by permission of Benchmark Books, Marshall Cavendish, New York.

The Art Lesson, by Tomie dePaola. Copyright © 1989 by Tomie dePaola. Reprinted by permission of G. P. Putnam's Sons, a division of Penguin Putnam Inc.

Brothers and Sisters, by Ellen B. Senisi. Copyright © 1993 by Ellen B. Senisi. Reprinted by permission of Scholastic Inc.

Carousel, by Pat Cummings. Copyright © 1994 by Pat Cummings. Reprinted by permission of Simon & Schuster Books for Young Readers, an imprint of Simon & Schuster Children's Publishing Division. All rights reserved.

The Great Ball Game: A Muskogee Story, retold by Joseph Bruchac, illustrated by Susan L. Roth. Text copyright © 1994 by Joseph Bruchac. Illustrations copyright © 1994 by Susan L. Roth. Reprinted by permission of Dial Books for Young Readers, a division of Penguin Putnam Inc.

Jalapeño Bagels, by Natasha Wing, illustrated by Robert Casilla. Text copyright © 1996 by Natasha Wing. Illustrations copyright © 1996 by Robert Casilla. Reprinted by permission of Simon & Schuster Books for Young Readers, an imprint of Simon & Schuster Children's Publishing Division. All rights reserved.

Moses Goes to a Concert, by Isaac Millman. Copyright © 1998 by Isaac Millman. Reprinted by permission of Farrar, Straus and Giroux, LLC.

Officer Buckle and Gloria, by Peggy Rathmann. Text and illustrations copyright © 1995 by Peggy Rathmann. All rights reserved. Reprinted by permission of G. P. Putnam's Sons, a division of Penguin Putnam Inc.

The School Mural, by Sarah Vázquez, illustrated by Melinda Levine. Copyright © 1998 Steck-Vaughn Company. Reprinted by permission from Steck-Vaughn Company. All rights reserved.

Thunder Cake, by Patricia Polacco. Copyright © 1990 by Patricia Polacco. All rights reserved. Reprinted by permission of Philomel Books, a division of Penguin Putnam Inc.

Links and Theme Openers

"Bat Attitude," by Lynn O'Donnell, from the October 1997 issue of *3 2 1 Contact* magazine. Copyright © 1997 by Children's Television Workshop. Reprinted by permission of the Children's Television Workshop.

"Calvin and Hobbes" comic strip from *The Indispensable Calvin & Hobbes*, by Bill Watterson. Copyright © by Bill Watterson. Reprinted with permission of Universal Press Syndicate. All rights reserved.

"Carousel," by Kathy Kranking, from the June 1998 issue of *Ranger Rick* magazine with the permission of the publisher, the National Wildlife Federation. Copyright © 1998 by the National Wildlife Federation.

"Do Not Enter" from *Oh, Grow Up!*, by Florence Parry Heide and Roxanne Heide Pierce, illustrated by Nadine Bernard Westcott. Text copyright © 1996 by Florence Parry Heide and Roxanne Heide Pierce. Reprinted by permission of Orchard Books, New York.

"Go to a Concert" from *Kids Make Music! Clapping & Tapping from Bach to Rock*, by Avery Hart and Paul Mantell. Copyright © 1993 by Avery Hart and Paul Mantell. Reprinted by permission of Williamson Publishing Company.

"I Did Not Eat Your Ice Cream" from *Something Big Has Been Here*, by Jack Prelutsky. Copyright © 1990 by Jack Prelutsky. Reprinted by permission of HarperCollins Publishers.

"Little Sister" from *Something On My Mind*, by Nikki Grimes. Copyright © 1978 by Nikki Grimes. Used by permission of Dial Books for Young Readers, a division of Penguin Putnam Inc.

"Peanuts Comic Strips" Two untitled comic strips by Charles M. Schulz. Peanuts copyright © United Feature Syndicate. Reprinted by permission of United Feature Syndicate.

"Sun & Ice" from *Out of the Bag: The Paper Bag Players Book of Plays,* by the Paper Bag Players. Text copyright © 1997 by the Paper Bag Players. Reprinted by permission of Hyperion Books for Children.

"Welcome to the Kitchen" from *Young Chef's Nutrition Guide and Cookbook,* by Carolyn Moore, Ph.D., R.D., Mimi Kerr, and Robert, Shulman, Ph.D. Copyright © 1990 by Barron's Educational Series, Inc. Reprinted by permission of Barrons Educational Series, Inc.

"What is a Family?" from *Fathers, Mothers, Sisters, Brothers: A Collection of Family Poems,* by Mary Ann Hoberman. Copyright © 1991 by Mary Ann Hoberman. Reprinted by permission of Little, Brown and Company (Inc.)

Credits

Photography

3 (b) Jens Rydell/Natural Selection. **7** Michael S. Yamashita/Corbis. **8** images Copyright © 2000 PhotoDisc, Inc. **18** Brooke Forsythe **52** Myrleen Ferguson/PhotoEdit. **54–5** Smithsonian National Postal Museum. **56** Corbis/Dan Guravich. **57** (t) Corbis/Dan Guravich. **60** (t) Remy Amann-Bios/Peter Arnold, Inc. (l) Zefa Germany/The Stock Market. (inset) Courtesy Marshall Cavendish. **60–1** (bkgd) J. A. Kraulis/MASTERFILE. **61** (inset) Raymond A. Mendez/AnimalsAnimals. **62–3** Hans Pfletschinger/Peter Arnold, Inc. **63** (r) Gary Retherford/NASC/Photo Researchers, Inc. **64** (t) Len Rue Jr. /NASC/Photo Researchers, Inc. (b) Jerome Wexler/NASC/Photo Researchers, Inc. **65** Leonard Lee Rue/NASC/Photo Researchers, Inc. **66–7** J. H. Robinson/NASC/Photo Researchers, Inc. **68** (t) Hans Pfletschinger/Peter Arnold, Inc. (b) Leonide Principe/NASC/Photo Researchers, Inc. **69** Rudolph Freund/NASC/Photo Researchers, Inc. **70** S. J. Krasemann/NASC/Photo Researchers, Inc. **71** John Dommers/NASC/Photo Researchers, Inc. **72** Gary Retherford/NASC/Photo Researchers, Inc. **73** (t) Philip K. Sharpe/Animals Animals. (b) S. J. Krasemann/Peter Arnold, Inc. **74** (l) K. G Preston-Mafham/Animals Animals. (r) Gregory D. Dimijian/NASC/Photo Researchers, Inc. **75** Gregory D. Dimijian/NASC/Photo Researchers, Inc. **76** Donald Specker/Animals Animals. **77** Mantis Wildlife Films, Oxford Scientific Films/Animals Animals. **78–9** Gary Retherford/NASC/Photo Researchers, Inc. **80–1** Hans Pfletschinger/Peter Arnold, Inc. **82–3** Varin/Jacana/NASC/Photo Researchers, Inc. **84** (inset) Raymond A. Mendez/Animals Animals. **85** (l) Bob Anderson/MASTERFILE. **84–5** (t) J. A. Kraulis/MASTERFILE. **88** (icon) image Copyright © 2000 PhotoDisc, Inc. **88–9** (bkgd) Ed Bock/The Stock Market. **89** (t) Corbis/Hulton-Deutsch Collection. (m) Seth Eastman/Wood River Gallery/PictureQuest. (b) Lawrence Migdale/Mira. **90** (t) Mike Greenlar/Mercury Pictures. (b) Courtesy Penguin Putnam. **111** (l) © Planet Earth Pictures 1998/FPG International. **112** (t) Jens Rydell/Natural Selection. **113** (l) Robin Thomas. (tr) John Serrao/Photo Researchers. (br) Corbis/Joe McDonald. **114–5** Stephen Dalton/Photo Researchers. **118** (icon) image Copyright © 2000 PhotoDisc, Inc. (t) Michael Paras/International Stock. (b) Rob Lewine/The Stock Market. **119** (tl) Ronnie Kaufman/The Stock Market. (tr) Zigy Kaluzny/Tony Stone Images. (bl) MTPA Stock/MASTERFILE. (br) Jon Riley/Tony Stone Images. **126–44** Ellen B. Senisi. **145** Mike Greenlar/Mercury Pictures. **146** Ellen B. Senisi. **147** (l) Courtesy Trisha Zembruski. (cl) Michael Newman/PhotoEdit. (cr) David Young-Wolff/PhotoEdit. **154** (t) StockByte. (b) John & Eliza Forder/Tony Stone Images. **154–5** Don Smetzer/Tony Stone Images. **155** Don Smetzer/Tony Stone Images. **156** (t) Courtesy Natasha Wing. (b) Tom Iannuzzi/Mercury Pictures. **184** Courtesy Pat Cummings. **218–21** Photographs © 1997 Christopher Hornsby. **222–3** Corbis Royalty Free. **224** Lawrence Migdale. **264–5** Michael S. Yamashita/Corbis. **266** NASA. **267** Roger Ressmeyer/Corbis. **268** (t) Corbis. (b) NASA. **269** Corbis. **270** (t) image Copyright © 2000 PhotoDisc, Inc. (b) NASA. **271** AFP/Corbis. **272** (bkgd) image Copyright © 2000 PhotoDisc, Inc. (b) Archive Photos/PictureQuest. **273** Corbis **274** (t) Dave G. Houser/Corbis. (b) Corbis/Bettmann. **275** Tom Bean/Corbis **276** (l) Kim Sayer/Corbis. (r) Wood River Gallery/PictureQuest. **277** (t) image Copyright

© 2000 PhotoDisc, Inc. (b) Jerry Cooke/Life Magazine © Time Inc. **278** Mark Kauffman/Life Magazine © Time Inc. **278–9** AP/Wide World Photos. **279** Corbis/Bettmann. **280** Corbis/Bettmann. **281** Corbis/Bettmann. **282** (t) Robert Maass/Corbis. (b) AP/Wide World Photos. **284** (icon) image Copyright © 2000 PhotoDisc, Inc. (bkgd) StockByte. **284–5** Eyewire. **291** (artwork) *Sunflowers,* Vincent Van Gogh, 1853–90, Dutch, National Gallery, London/SuperStock. **319** © 1997 Suki Couglin. **322–3** *Tamalada (Making Tamales),* 1987. Carmen Lomas Garza. **324** *Guacamole,* 1989. Carmen Lmoas Garza. gouache, 9 x 5 1/2 inches, Collection of Antonia Castaneda and Arturo Madrid, Claremont, CA. **325** *Naranjas (Oranges),* 1990. Carmen Lomas Garza. **326** Corbis Royalty Free. **328** Dave Schlabowske/TIME Inc. **330** Tom Ianuzzi/Mercury Pictures. **366** image Copyright © 2000 PhotoDisc, Inc. **367** Rick Friedman/Black Star/PictureQuest. **368–9** Oliver Benn/Tony Stone Images. **370–1** Jeffry W. Myers/IndexStock. **393** (t) John Redmond. (b) Kenneth Rice Photography. **400** PhotoSpin. **401** Dick Luria/FPG International. **402** (l) image Copyright © 2000 PhotoDisc, Inc. **403** Artville. **404** Artville. **405** Digital Vision/PictureQuest. **406** Corbis Royalty Free. **407** image Copyright © 2000 PhotoDisc, Inc. **409** Corbis Royalty Free. **410** Donna Day/Tony Stone Images.

Ulrich. **372** (inset) **373–392** Melinda Levine. **393, 394** (b) **395** Jim Kelly.

Assignment Photography
16–7, 180–1, 258–61, 291, 329, 365 (r) Joel Benjamin. **53, 85** (r), **111, 147** (r), **156–7** (bkgd), **178–9, 217, 257, 321, 395** Ken Karp. **117, 263, 399** Tony Scarpetta.

Illustration
10–11 Copyright © 2001 by Lori Lohstoeter. **58–59** Carolyn Iverson. **84** Mike Reed. **86** William Brinkley & Associates. **86-87** Nancy Gibson-Nash. **124–125** Dave Klug. **148–149** Eric Brace. **150–151** Copyright © 2001 by Raúl Colón. **156, 178** Tom Brenner. **183** Clive Scruton. **184** (c), **216** (c), (b) **217** (t) Eileen Gilbride. **224, 256, 257** Jason Farris. **319, 320** (c) (bl) Daniel Del Valle. **330, 364** (b) **365** George